P9-CJF-654

# PRAISE FOR *COME AND EAT*

"Funny, thought-provoking, and totally real, Bri writes in a way that makes you feel like you are sitting down in your comfiest pajamas with your oldest and dearest friend. *Come and Eat* inspired me in ways I never expected—I literally could not put it down. It's a message every woman needs to hear . . . even (perhaps especially) if you hate to cook!"

—**RUTH SOUKUP**, *New York Times* bestselling author
of *Living Well, Spending Less* and *Unstuffed*

"The first thing I noticed about Bri is that she has a smile that takes over her whole body and immediately makes you feel welcomed into her life. *Come and Eat* gives you basically that same exact feeling. In these days when everyone seems to be in such a hurry and too busy for real community and deep relationships, Bri invites us into her story of discovering the importance of fellowship around something as simple as the dinner table. You will be inspired to gather the people you know—and the people you have yet to really know—around your table to experience a little bit of God's kingdom right here on Earth."

—**MELANIE SHANKLE**, *New York Times* bestselling author and speaker

"*Come and Eat* is an invitation to every hungry heart who's craving faith and love with a sprinkle of holy adventure. Bri is a vibrant, welcoming hostess who serves up truth and grace in equal measures. You'll finish this book both full and longing for another helping."

—**HOLLEY GERTH**, bestselling author of *You're Already Amazing*

"Bri shares stories and recipes—not only to nourish our bodies but to nourish our hearts and prepare a place for deep connection. Bri is one of the most beautiful and genuine women I know. Her words will give you insights and inspiration in the kitchen and around the table. This book is a recipe for cultivating deep and life-changing relationships."

—**LISA LEONARD**, founder of Lisa Leonard Designs

"A coveted place at Bri's table also means she has made a loving space for you in her heart. In this book, with unbound generosity, Bri shares both table and heart with all of us."

—**JOY WILSON**, author of *Joy the Baker's Over Easy*

Received On:

OCT 16 2017

THIS IS Fremont Library LIBRA
THE SEATTLE PUBLIC

"With every page of *Come and Eat* I felt as though Bri was welcoming me to her table and we were having a fabulous meal together. Her transparency made me feel loved and not alone in this world. This book is a breath of fresh air, breathing life into something I believe in with all my heart: sharing meals together transforms lives."

—**JAMIE IVEY**, host of *The Happy Hour with Jamie Ivey* podcast, author of *If You Only Knew: My Unlikely, Unavoidable Story of Becoming Free*

"I love how Bri invites us to see the world through someone else's eyes—whether we're getting on a plane to go and serve abroad or standing in our kitchens serving up dinner to our neighbors."

—**LISA-JO BAKER**, bestselling author of *Never Unfriended* and community manager for (in)courage

"Bri takes the best of life—neighbors, good food, the hope of Christ—and cooks it down into an invitation to reach for the solace of community. I'll be holding on to *Come and Eat*, both for the go-to recipes and for the reminder that God's love for me is a feast best shared with those around me."

—**SHANNAN MARTIN**, author of *Falling Free: Rescued from the Life I Always Wanted*

"Absolutely beautiful—an inspiring, challenging, comforting reminder that ultimately our tables are about so much more than food. Bri's stories are delightful, her recipes are scrumptious, and her approach to building and strengthening community around the table is refreshingly practical. More than anything, though, *Come and Eat* is a call to 'taste and see that the Lord is good' (Psalm 34:8), to gather around the table, join hands, pursue peace, and celebrate His unfathomable, unending grace. What a gift."

—**SOPHIE HUDSON**, author of *Giddy Up, Eunice* and cohost of *The Big Boo Cast*

"The invitation that Bri extends through *Come and Eat* is so equally inspiring and practical that we simply won't see our dinner tables the same again. With honesty, insightfulness, and a call to action, Bri shows us we can make an impact right where we are, around the table."

—**RUTH CHOU SIMONS**, artist and author of *GraceLaced: Discovering Timeless Truths Through Seasons of the Heart*, founder of GraceLaced.com

# Come and Eat

### A CELEBRATION *of* LOVE *and* GRACE AROUND *the* EVERYDAY TABLE

## BRI MCKOY

NELSON
BOOKS

An Imprint of Thomas Nelson

© 2017 by Brianne McKoy

All rights reserved. No portion of this book may be reproduced, stored in a retrieval system, or transmitted in any form or by any means—electronic, mechanical, photocopy, recording, scanning, or other—except for brief quotations in critical reviews or articles, without the prior written permission of the publisher.

Published in Nashville, Tennessee, by Nelson Books, an imprint of Thomas Nelson. Nelson Books and Thomas Nelson are registered trademarks of HarperCollins Christian Publishing, Inc.

Thomas Nelson titles may be purchased in bulk for educational, business, fund-raising, or sales promotional use. For information, please e-mail SpecialMarkets@ThomasNelson.com.

Any Internet addresses, phone numbers, or company or product information printed in this book are offered as a resource and are not intended in any way to be or to imply an endorsement by Thomas Nelson, nor does Thomas Nelson vouch for the existence, content, or services of these sites, phone numbers, companies, or products beyond the life of this book.

Unless otherwise noted, Scripture quotations are taken from the ESV® Bible (The Holy Bible, English Standard Version®), copyright © 2001 by Crossway, a publishing ministry of Good News Publishers. Used by permission. All rights reserved.

Scripture quotations marked NIV are taken from the Holy Bible, New International Version®, NIV®. Copyright © 1973, 1978, 1984, 2011 by Biblica, Inc.™ Used by permission of Zondervan. All rights reserved worldwide. www.zondervan.com. The "NIV"and "New International Version" are trademarks registered in the United States Patent and Trademark Office by Biblica, Inc.™

Scripture quotations marked THE MESSAGE are from *The Message.* Copyright © by Eugene H. Peterson 1993, 1994, 1995, 1996, 2000, 2001, 2002. Used by permission of Tyndale House Publishers, Inc.

Scripture quotations marked NASB are from the New American Standard Bible®, Copyright © 1960, 1962, 1963, 1968, 1971, 1972, 1973, 1975, 1977, 1995 by The Lockman Foundation. Used by permission. (www.Lockman.org)

### Library of Congress Cataloging-in-Publication Data

Names: McKoy, Bri, 1984-author.
Title: Come and eat: a celebration of love and grace around the everyday
    table / Bri McKoy.
Description: Nashville, Tennessee: Nelson Books, [2017] | Includes
    bibliographical references.
Identifiers: LCCN 2017007194 | ISBN 9780718090616
Subjects: LCSH: Hospitality—Religious aspects—Christianity. | Dinners and
    dining—Religious aspects—Christianity.
Classification: LCC BV4647.H67 M35 2017 | DDC 241/.671—dc23 LC record available at
https://lccn.loc.gov/2017007194

*Printed in the United States of America*

17 18 19 20 21 LSC 6 5 4 3 2 1

*For Jesus. For not only giving me a story
to write, but a story to live.*

# CONTENTS

*"True hospitality is marked by an open response to the dignity of each and every person."*

—KATHLEEN NORRIS

# INTRODUCTION

I did not grow up learning to cook. If you had looked for me as a child, you wouldn't have found me in the kitchen beside my mom. More likely you'd have found me with my face firmly stuck in some book. This state of general unfamiliarity with the kitchen continued into my adult years. As a young woman just starting out on my own, I relied heavily on my ability to put a salad together for lunches at work and then often ate out for dinner. Meals were more a physical necessity than an intentionally planned-out custom of significance. I figured I'd always have time to learn my way around the kitchen later, perhaps whenever I got married. But then 2011 came, I made a forever commitment to my husband, Jeremy, and suddenly "later" became today.

The image I had in my mind for my first entrance into the kitchen as a new wife was quite picturesque: a gorgeous stiff white apron, my hair perfectly pulled back, my smile taut and confident. In this scenario, I wore high heels, because in my imagination I was an extremely sexy cook. But as is so often the case, reality was not quite in line with what I had envisioned. If I'm honest, my first steps into the kitchen were less like steps and more like reluctant kicks followed by screaming. You would have thought I was being asked to enter a horror house. And I scare easily.

That first year of marriage, the only thing that got me past my dread of the kitchen was knowing I could pick up the phone and call my mom. The hours I clocked on the phone with my mom were world-class status. She came to be my very own living *Joy of Cooking* resource. I'd ask her about spices and vegetables and perfect temperatures to cook meat and the best way to brown a roast. It occurred to me at some point, through my endless questions, that while I had grown up eating my mom's unforgettable meals at our family table, I had never really paid attention to the crucial act of cooking. I was about to learn how little I truly knew when I attempted to make an onion casserole.

Leaning over our tiny kitchen countertop, I wildly flipped through a cooking magazine, looking for a recipe. Instead of my earlier vision of starched apron and high heels, I was in workout clothes, which would have been completely reasonable except for the fact that I had not been to the gym at all that day. Or that whole week. My hair was in a wild messy bun with stray tendrils escaping the loose top knot. There was salsa on my shirt due to my nervous snacking while trying to figure out if it would be okay to have hot dogs for a fourth night in a row. I was one hot mess.

Determined to rise above, I continued to search furiously for a recipe that seemed at least remotely doable. Most of the recipes in the magazine called for ingredients I did not have, which immediately disqualified them, but then my eyes landed on one for onion casserole. Definitely a possibility. After all, I had all the ingredients. Brilliant! How could I go wrong? Of course, wrong was the only turn I would take with this meal. The recipe called exclusively for somewhere around ten onions, heavy cream, and salt and pepper.

I happened to have a bag of onions, so, in sheer excitement, I began chopping. The whole process was deliriously satisfying. *Look at me, I am a cook!* I felt like a hunter and gatherer. I had found a recipe, and now I was making it. Tears poured down my cheeks as I chopped what seemed like my hundredth onion, but it did not bother me because all I could think was, *I did it. I have arrived.* I was so impressed with myself that I pondered slipping on some high heels—you know, to complement my yoga pants.

The thing about learning how to cook is that learning how to choose a good recipe is an incredibly important part of the process, and I was woefully untrained. This is how foreign the skill of cooking was to me: I thought onions baked with cream would be an irresistible feast!

Later that evening, Jeremy came home, and I pulled the casserole out of the oven, as if to say, "Look at me! I am woman and chef extraordinaire!" I cut a slice and watched as the diced onions poured over the spoon while the heavy cream pooled at the bottom of the baking dish. It looked very unappetizing, but I was blinded by my great accomplishment. It took all of one bite for my lofty pride to come melting down into that dish with the cream. It. Was. Awful.

It tasted like a spoonful of pungent onions with the cream desperately trying, but failing, to tame the sharp taste. I remember looking up at Jeremy, almost in shock, realizing that the onion casserole **TASTED. LIKE. ONIONS.** That was it. My eyes, not yet fully recovered from the tears they'd shed while I chopped the onions, started to wet themselves again.

Jeremy, in his sweet, gentle way, took my hand and said, "Babe, this does not taste good." We burst out laughing. We ordered pizza. Then we both held the baking dish and watched the soupy onions fall into the trash can. To the credit of the person who wrote the recipe, I'm sure it was not meant to be the main dish. But I was still learning to understand food, how to read a recipe, how to know what ingredients work well with one another, and how to pull it all together into a delicious meal.

Over that year I did learn to cook. In fact, I didn't just learn to cook; I fell in love with cooking. One and a half years into marriage, Jeremy presented me with diamond earrings for my birthday. Once I clarified that they were, in fact, real diamond earrings, I promptly returned them and purchased pots and pans. Cooking became an outlet and my art.

But something else also happened in those first few years of marriage. While my cooking skills increased, our presence at the table diminished. It wasn't that we didn't *want* to regularly gather around our table as much as it was life getting in the way. It was a combination of so many things. It was the difficulty of those first few years of marriage. It was growing up. It was learning to be a responsible and loving citizen of the world. It was keeping up with a demanding job. It was realizing that my relationship with God also took work. It was chores and grocery shopping (my number-one disliked task forever and ever. Amen).

Inevitably, at the end of each day, right around mealtime, I was already completely poured out. For a while coming to the table seemed like one last push before I could clock out from the day. But what I would come to learn is that sharing a meal at the table isn't so much another thing to check off my list as it is an invitation from God to see his goodness and rejoice in his work before surrendering to the night. It's about rescuing relationships and partnering with God to show more of his love to a hurting world. It's about discovering that perhaps before we invite people to meet Jesus at church or at Christian events, we should invite them to meet him at our table. It's about honoring what God has already given us to bring his kingdom down to earth. It's about looking at an invitation to come and eat as an entryway to God's ultimate invitation to be redeemed and rescued by him.

In its simplest form, it's about mirroring how Jesus chose to enter this world and show his love to the people who needed him so desperately. In fact, it's amazing how often the Bible records Jesus showing up at a table to share a meal, and furthermore, how many times Jesus himself extended the invitation to come and eat.

> Jesus said to them, "Come and have breakfast." Now none of the disciples dared ask him, "Who are you?" They knew it was the Lord. (John 21:12)

> Come, everyone who thirsts,
>    come to the waters;
> and he who has no money,
>    *come, buy and eat*!
> Come, buy wine and milk
>    without money and without price. (Isaiah 55:1,
>       emphasis mine)

> The Spirit and the Bride say, "Come." And let the one who hears say, "Come." And let the one who is thirsty come; let the one who desires take the water of life without price. (Revelation 22:17)

What if there is more power in the simple invitation to come and eat than we can even begin to fathom? What if, in sharing a meal, in our eating and our drinking with others, we truly can proclaim the good news? What if the most accessible and consistent way we can share the love of Jesus with others is right in our home? Right around our very own common dining room table?

*one*

# A LIFETIME OF TABLES

*You prepare a table before me . . .*

PSALM 23:5

Food has manifested itself in my life in many diverse forms. Food as a peace offering. Food as celebration. Food as comfort. However, perhaps ironically, food and I got off to a terrible start.

My mom had me a few weeks late. The way she tells it, I just wasn't ready to come into this world. But a womb can only bear another soul for so long. So with my mother's hot and weary efforts and the forceps in the doctor's hands, I was literally pushed and then pulled into the world. I came with one blown-out lung, which promptly progressed into two deflated lungs. For three months, doctors poked and prodded and conjectured over me. And my mom, she labored over me, this time not to bring me into life but

1

to sustain my life. I've heard, once you have a child, the laboring never ends.

I look back on my baby pictures and see what looks like a science project. Tubes weaving in and out of my body. Needles in too many veins to count. And a little broken body that couldn't eat. Everything that went in promptly came back up. It seemed almost as if I were on a hunger strike. Like I knew something of this busted-up world I was entering, and I was wondering if I could commit to doing life in this foreign land.

It's hard for me to believe that, as a newborn, I didn't have some real and unexplainable sense of where I had come from, of who God is, seeing as we are told in Psalm 139 that he forms us in the womb. I once read a story about a mom who walked into her baby's room to find her three-year-old son in the room with the baby, standing by her crib just watching her. When the mom asked her son what he was doing, he said, "Trying not to forget what Jesus feels like." I think in our own quiet ways, we're all trying not to forget what Jesus feels like.

But we enter this world. We come unable to express ourselves with words or even actions. Everything we do must be interpreted. When asked, most new parents say that the first few months of their newborn's life is all eating and sleeping. Unless you're my parents, in which case it was all crying and rejecting everything. Especially food.

For most babies, their first introduction to food in this world is intimate. If it does not take place at the mother's breast, it takes place while being held. A baby's first table isn't some beautiful whitewashed wooden structure. It's skin. Nestled by the belly, rocked by the rhythm of the beating heart. Secured by loving arms. It is just like God to plan it this way, to have us enter the world with mouths open, hungry. Receiving food from the body of the one who bore us.

It's designed to be an intimate experience. Satisfying. And, I am thinking, God intends the tables throughout life to be just as cherished. Sharing a meal together with someone can be deeply personal. If you take the time to feed another person, if you nourish their body, they naturally start to reveal their heart. Food is the answer to a basic need, and it can become a gateway to *the* need: redemption from a loving Savior.

Hunger runs deep in us, deeper than we fully grasp sometimes. Jesus saw this hunger, so when he came to this earth, he spent time in our homes. At our tables. He fed us fish and loaves of bread and wine overflowing. While we gnawed on our crusty loaf, he told us we'd need more than just bread. We're more than just hungry. Then, as his ultimate act of feeding us, he broke his body just like he broke that bread and said, "Here, eat my body and drink my blood, and you will never thirst or want again." It's visceral. It's us reaching for him and partaking of his life. He showed us that sometimes we are hungry for food, but sometimes hunger is a signal. It's a longing for something, or Someone, more. He still invites us today: "Behold, I stand at the door and knock. If anyone hears my voice and opens the door, I will come in to him and eat with him, and he with me" (Revelation 3:20).

The connection between the saving work of Jesus and the meals we share is such a thing of beauty and wonder to me now, but this wasn't always the case. Seeing as my body was on wild revolt when I entered the world, my relationship with food was initially broken. As a direct result, I've been small in stature my whole life. When I was ten I found myself back in a hospital being poked and prodded again. My body didn't seem to want to grow up. But I gradually learned to love my petiteness, to understand it as a battle wound. The wound I received when I was trying to stay in the presence of Jesus, in the safety of the womb where he created me.

Jesus knew exactly what he was doing when he placed me in my mom's body. She comes from a long line of cooks and bakers, and even though I initially rejected food like I was rejecting the evil of the world, she spent much of her life making up for my rocky start by feeding me some of the best meals I've ever had. She'd sit me at her table and show me the wonder of food.

Through the years of my mom's tireless commitment to cooking weeknight meals and inviting our family to come and eat, I started to realize that my connection to God had not been completely severed when I entered this world. I found him in my family's mealtime conversations. I found him while sharing late-night nachos with a friend at her table. Every time I'd pull up a chair to a table, I'd discover it was a sacred time, a holy place. I was learning that if I wanted to love like Christ, showing up to the table was the best place to start.

**TIP:** A great first step to creating a culture of sharing regular meals at the table is to choose three or four days a week your family can agree on and put them on the family calendar so everyone can plan ahead. You can reevaluate the best days for meals around the table every week.

Since those earlier days, I've eaten at so many kinds of tables. For me, a table is so much more than a physical piece of furniture; it's everything that happens around it that gives it such transcending significance. The form the table takes is of little importance. It can be a picnic table, a beach towel laid out on the shores of white sand, the wooden floor of a tree house, or the carpet of a friend's living room. If the purpose of that area is to gather around a meal, I immediately recognize it as a table.

And the food never has to be extravagant, because the person at the table always is. The meal can be as simple as a feast of sweet, tangy oranges washed down with crisp water. Or chunky, fresh salsa dipped and even double dipped (oh yes!) with crunchy chips. We don't have to overthink things to partake in the multifaceted beauty of the table; that's what I'm learning.


We will have the honor of sitting around so many different tables in our lifetimes.

My favorite table so far has been one I had the privilege to sit at in Thailand. I was there for two months with a group of girls doing mission work. For the first week, we stayed at the pastor's house in a tiny village known for leprosy. Fourteen of us rolled out our sleeping bags every night in a small playroom, and in the morning, we'd roll our beds back up to make room for the kids who gathered every day for Bible school. The days were long and hot. We didn't get much sleep, and I think we were particularly drained by the realization of how devastating life was for so many of the villagers, several of whom were plagued with leprosy. But each evening the pastor's wife would put together slats of wood as a table. It was only about one foot off the ground. She would lay pillows on the floor and then cook us the best Thai meals I have ever eaten to this day.

The first course was always steaming soup. A clear broth so hot that when we dropped in a few shoots of raw vegetables, they were instantly poached and flavored by the juice. This soup went down savory and finished with a touch of spice. Then, just like that, a parade of Thailand's best meals seemed to magically appear out of that tiny kitchen.

The pastor's wife had just one stove with one burner and one big pot. To this day, I'm not sure how such amazing and bountiful food came out of her kitchen. Feeding all fourteen of us was no small task, but she did it every night for one week. She served us pad thai piled high and studded with the freshest cilantro. She made basil chicken so aromatic and savory that I ached for it even while I was eating it, knowing I would probably never taste anything like it again. Dessert was always sticky rice with mangos that we peeled right there at the table, the syrupy juice running down our hands and slathered onto our every taste bud. Those meals were a bright light amid some dark days. They were the reminder of God's provision, the strength that took us from emptiness to "we can do it again tomorrow."

One of the saddest tables I've ever sat around was in a hotel lobby after the funeral of a young friend. So many of us gathered from all over the country, and we pulled tables and chairs from every corner of that building together into one big gathering. We ate cold pizza and drank warm soda and toasted to one of the best we'd ever known. Our sobs crescendoed into laughter and then back to sobs. The tables we had puzzle-pieced together seemed to make us brave, and we gripped the sides while asking questions we would never find answers to. It was a safe place for us to let the tears flow, and then just moments later it acted as a stage as we each tried to do our best impressions of the friend who'd always made us laugh. Ultimately, those worn hotel lobby tables gave us a place to gather and melted us down to our truest selves: children of God. They made us family.

Then there was my best friend's wedding table. I sat at her reception and raised my champagne glass to all the many blessings being poured on her and her new husband. I ate the wedding feast and forked up bites of cake in between dancing and chatting. And then she got into her car with her new husband and drove away, at which moment I collapsed and heaved big tears, thinking of all the ways our relationship would now be different, what with me being still single and living states away. The other bridesmaids rushed me back into the wedding venue and quickly made a place for me at a vacant table. They fed me more cake while I unraveled. They prepared a table for me.

I look back on that memory, and it seems a little odd at first, that I would erupt into tears right there in front of everyone as the bride and groom made their exit, and that the safest place my friends knew to usher me to was a table. But something about the steadiness of the chair and my elbows braced against the table made me remember that it was all going to be okay. My friends joining me at the table with cake and jokes to make me smile reminded me that God was still with me and his plan was good.

God has no limit to the tables he will seat us around in our lifetimes. Tables of sorrow and brokenness. Tables of joy and celebration. Tables of everydayness. I believe with all my heart that we all have at least one life-defining moment that has happened around a table. Look at Jesus' life here on this earth. So many life-defining moments for him (and life-defining moments for all of humanity) happened around a table. The gospel of Luke barely shows Jesus in a scene where he is not eating, or at a table, or on his way to a meal. In fact, Jesus ate so much that in Luke 7:34 we find him being accused of being a glutton and a drunkard.

Could we have predicted that the Savior of the world would come and eat so much? That he would appear in our homes, at our tables? That some of his greatest lessons and hardest truths would spill out around a table, over a meal? It's so preposterous. It's so completely average. But how could he not? Jesus left the comforts of heaven and came down in human flesh to save all of humanity. And he happened to find us, eating. At a table. It's clear Jesus knew something about the power of a meal. It's clear that for him it wasn't as much about what was placed on the table as who was placed at the table.

The ministry of a meal didn't begin with Jesus' life on this earth. God modeled it long before that. Let's look at the Old Testament prophet Elijah, for example. He worked tirelessly on God's behalf, healing and performing miracles and proclaiming the one true God. But at one point in his journey, he learned that Jezebel, a hateful queen, wanted to have him killed. This was his breaking point, and Elijah fled into the desert. How often have we faced our own end-of-rope moments and retreated into the desert of doubt and hopelessness? But God had great compassion on Elijah and ministered to him first through a meal.

> And behold, an angel touched him [Elijah] and said to him, "Arise and eat." And he looked, and behold, there was at his head a cake baked on hot stones and a jar of water. And he ate and drank and lay down again. And the angel of the LORD came again a second time and touched him and said, "Arise and eat, for the journey is too great for you." And he arose and ate and drank, and went in the strength of that food forty days and forty nights to Horeb, the mount of God. (1 Kings 19:5–8)

God prepared a table for Elijah in the desert. He met Elijah's basic need first with a meal, and it opened the door for Elijah to journey to the mount of God and speak honestly and openly with God. Can a meal be the strengthening for our journey into the heart of God? Can a meal give us the durability to speak candidly and vulnerably to the living God? And is God preparing tables all around us because he wants us to approach him? To commune with him? Do we believe that in all seasons God is preparing a table for us, if only to draw us near?

If God strengthened his people by first feeding them and then Jesus came, flesh and blood, and revealed himself to us by entering our homes and eating with us, maybe a meal is more powerful than we have ever imagined. Maybe we should start looking more intently at the tables God is preparing before us.

In a generation of individualism, high shrubs and fences, fast meals, and fierce independence, the call to come and eat is needed now more than ever. Will you come with me and pull up a chair as we explore the power of the table? Let's look more closely together at how Jesus used his time over a meal to teach and heal and extend great compassion and mercy. How he chose to change the world by starting inside our homes, at our tables.

## PRAYER FOR THE TABLE

*Jesus, thank you. Thank you for meeting us exactly where we are. In our own homes, at our own tables. Thank you for meeting our basic need so that we can have a window into our deepest need: your saving grace. May we receive not just this food we are about to eat but also your great love. The love that provides. The love that prepares a place for us at the table. Amen.*

## QUESTIONS FOR THE TABLE

1. Take time to reflect on all the different tables God has placed you at over the years. Share a favorite memory from a meal you have had.
2. What was so amazing about that meal? Was it the food? Or the people? Was it the conversation? Or just the way you felt?
3. What are your thoughts on how many times Jesus appeared at a meal in the Gospels? Is this new to you? Why do you think it is significant?
4. Is there anyone in your life right now who, like Elijah, might be at the end of his or her rope? Plan as a family to take a meal to that person or to invite him or her over to share a meal with you.

## RECIPE FOR THE TABLE

# THE EASIEST AND TASTIEST ROAST

---

**Serves 5 to 6.**

*Think of this recipe as a kickoff to your journey of coming to the table consistently and enjoying a meal with the people you love. It's the easiest recipe I have in my arsenal, and my friends have told me time and time again that it's one of the tastiest roasts they've had. The simplicity of this recipe is a great reminder to me that the focus at the table is not the meal. It's the people.*

## Ingredients:
1 (3-pound) chuck roast
1/2 teaspoon salt
1/4 teaspoon pepper
1 tablespoon olive oil
1 (16-ounce) jar pepperoncinis
5 whole garlic cloves, peeled

## Instructions:
Pat the roast dry. Season with salt and pepper on all sides.

Optional: Brown the roast before adding it to your slow cooker. Heat a large skillet over medium-high heat. Add the olive oil. When the oil is shimmering, add the roast, and brown it on each side for 1 to 2 minutes.

Add the roast to a slow cooker. Pour the whole jar of pepperoncinis, including the juice, over the roast. Add the garlic cloves. Cover and cook on low for 8 hours or on high for 4 hours. The meat is done when it easily shreds with a fork.

*Alternate cooking method: Dutch Oven*

I like to cook this roast in my Dutch oven when I can. I do this so I can brown the roast before adding all the ingredients (which gives it great flavor), and because I love using my Dutch oven!

Preheat the oven to 325 degrees.

Season the roast on all sides with salt and pepper.

Heat a Dutch oven over medium-high heat. Add the olive oil. When the oil is shimmering, add the roast, and brown it on each side (1 to 2 minutes per side).

Remove the Dutch oven from the heat. Add the whole jar of pepperoncinis, with the juice, and the garlic cloves. Cover with the lid, and bake for 3 hours.

To see images of this meal, visit http://oursavorylife.com/the-easiest-paleo-roast-recipe/.

TRICK ———————————————————————————————

"Pot roast" is not a specific cut of meat. You can't go to the grocery store and find "pot roast" in the meat department. The term itself refers to a method for taking tough meat and cooking it low and slow until it is juicy and falling apart. So you can use any kind of tough meat. My recommendation for a perfect pot roast: chuck roast.

# two

# A PLACE FOR US AT THE TABLE

*She had a sister called Mary, who sat at the*
*Lord's feet listening to what he said.*

LUKE 10:39 NIV

The table Jesus invites me to most often is the table in my own home. This table is so utterly normal, so perfectly unassuming. I walk by it a thousand times a day. I throw mail at it and scrap pieces of paper and pens and thoughts. It has a large crack in it that makes me both love and hate it. This is the table I must choose to join every day, the table the Lord prepares for me. But the truth is, even though Jesus invites me to this table almost every evening, I often uninvite myself.

Most days by the time five o'clock rolls around, I want to shut it all down. I don't want to talk about my day because it's still fresh like wet paint—do not touch. I start to dismantle my sanity. I want fluffy slippers and a bucket of my favorite beverage—yes, a bucket. I start to think seriously about the cost of a personal chef (which, Jeremy tells me, will never be in our budget). Second choice would be paying a visit to the closest taco truck. Excuse me, but I think we *can* live on tacos alone. Salsa is a food group that I place at the top, middle, and bottom of the food pyramid!

This is not the vision I have for dinner when my morning starts. In fact, I usually start my day feeling hopeful. I kiss Jeremy goodbye as he leaves for work and get excited about when he will come home. I think about the dinner I am going to make and how we will sit at the table and have intelligent, life-transforming conversations. I picture us coming to the table joyful and so grateful for the full day we have just lived. Maybe we'll do an inductive Bible study or spend our time in prayer. This is where I'm at when it's bright and early, with two cups of coffee coursing through me and an awareness of the Holy Spirit living in me, fresh and new and nearly tangible.

But this scene I play in my head, the one about the beautiful meal at the end of the day, never—and I mean never!—happens. Because by the end of the day my job and responsibilities and to-do lists have taken everything I have and all those things I didn't even think I had. The day is drawing to a close and I'm empty. I'm angry or hurt because that friend didn't call. Or that meeting at work did not go as planned. Then my husband comes home. Late. And I'm just not having it anymore.

At 7:00 a.m. I was sure Jeremy and I would close out the day at the table over a mouthwatering meal and such enticing conversation that we'd fall in love all over again. We'd laugh endearingly at how smart and easy our conversation was while delicately wiping the sides of our mouths. Instead, the reality is that by 7:00 p.m., I'm wiping the humanity of my husband clean off with harsh words and crushed dreams. I'm discouraged by how little I actually accomplished and how much I failed. I cannot figure out adulthood or sainthood or anything in between. I can't even make a meal.

And so I start to excuse myself from my own dinner table before I even arrive. In so doing, I unknowingly uninvite others too, like Jeremy, or my neighbors, who I know get home late from work. Or the couple I see sitting on the bench right across my street every single day.

For a time, it felt like my longing for a consistent meal at the table and the reality of my life could never merge. Whenever Jeremy and I *did* come to the table, it was uncomfortable and quiet. We asked the same questions—questions we already knew the answers to. The truth was, we both had demanding jobs. We both traveled a lot. When we were at our freshest (mid-morning), we weren't even together. We were only getting about three to four hours with each other every evening, and those hours happened to be when we were both at our most tired. The breaking point for us? When we realized we'd forgotten each other. For the sake of our marriage, we needed to change the game.

I can tell you now from our own experience that the consequences of not meeting at the table are severe. When Jeremy and I were struggling with this, we found ourselves eating out more. Because we were eating out more, a larger portion of our budget was going toward that expense. On top of that, we were not connecting in conversation, because, even when we brought the food home, it was easier to eat our takeout in front of the television. We were going to bed emotionally empty, and we were not getting restful sleep.

Once we were awakened to the problem of our routine, I started looking into what seemed to be at the root—not coming to the table—and found some startling statistics. In my research,

I found that family meals are on a steep decline. While the consistent act of gathering at the table is becoming a disappearing act, almost everything shattering our world is on the rise: teen suicide, depression, divorce, violence, bullying, addiction. Could it be that getting back to the table inside our own homes could have an undeniable impact on the world outside our doors? One study that I found particularly jolting was from the National Center on Addiction and Substance Abuse at Columbia University. This study found that kids and teens who share family dinners three or more times per week

- perform better academically,
- are less likely to engage in risky behaviors (drugs, alcohol, sexual activity), and
- have better relationships with their parents.[1]

Even though we did not yet have kids, these statistics were sobering. It occurred to me that reaping the benefits of coming to the table did not have to be delayed until we had kids. It could start with us wherever we were right then. A meal at the table was more important than I had previously suspected.

As I continued exploring the impact of meals at the table, I also started to notice all the times in Scripture when Jesus was at a table or sharing a meal. I read through Luke and found that Jesus very clearly and consistently modeled for us the importance of coming to the table. I started to believe, and then experience, that consistent meals at the table can be linked to saving marriages, enriching relationships, practicing gratitude, saving us money, keeping us healthy, and encouraging us to love our neighbors.

It was a life-changing revelation, which, if true, made the transition from couch to table imperative. This meant some changes for Jeremy and me. I started making quicker meals, even though

I had learned to adore creating in the kitchen for hours on end by that point. This meant less of my energy was spent on cooking, and it also meant less cleanup. Jeremy, on the other hand, committed to coming home consistently at a regular time. That way we could maximize the hours we *did* have together, and we'd both know our priorities were aligned.

While these key changes helped get us to the table, we also realized that we had to change what we brought to the table. The stale questions weren't doing it for us anymore, but we were often too tired to think of the questions that spark. So we got help. We bought books. And we got creative with our selections! One of our first was a textbook on food and drink pairing, because this is something we love and wanted to learn more about. We also bought a humorous book on marriage (*The Antelope in the Living Room* by Melanie Shankle) and another one full of questions we could use to jump-start conversation.

Some nights we'd go through the food-pairing book, which was fascinating because I started to relearn how Jeremy takes in information, how he studies and interprets what's before him, and he relearned the same about me. Other nights we'd read a few paragraphs from *The Antelope in the Living Room*. This one was a favorite because Melanie is such a great storyteller and her own stories on marriage made Jeremy and me both feel lighter and less crazy! And then on other nights, we'd follow some of the prompts from the Q&A book to get some fresh conversation flowing. All these different resources we employed helped us to forget about the workday and instead laugh, reminisce, and jump into the depths of interesting thoughts we might not have had otherwise. Reading together reminded us of the things we loved about each other while we were still dating, and we relished every moment. Quite simply, we started making a place for our marriage—and, really, ourselves—at our own table.

Here's what I've learned and am still learning about the table: it is a wondrous place. It is the rabbit hole in Alice's Wonderland just beckoning for us to fall down it—and to bring friends and loved ones and stories along with us. And if the traditional meal at the table isn't working (setting the table, lavish meals, solemn prayer, conversations about the day), then it must be changed. Nothing says a meal at the table has to look a certain way. Bring a game to the table. Do a casual night with a cheese board once a week. Eat off paper plates with plastic spoons, and place it all on a disposable tablecloth so you can throw everything away at the end of the night if the mess is causing stress. Better yet, do it with parchment paper and crayons. Come to the table in pajamas! Amen.

What will it take to make a place for yourself at your own everyday table? A place you want to show up to?

Once we learn to practice the art of coming consistently to our own table, we will also be able to create space for ourselves at other tables. These are the tables outside our homes that are begging for our presence and participation. These are the tables Jesus asks us to go sit around.

Jesus was, without shame, an expert at finding a place for himself in others' homes. He wasn't afraid of entering into the lives and worlds of others, places that were perhaps more comfortable for the people he was looking to reach. On many accounts, he did not wait for an invitation but invited himself. One day as Jesus was entering Jericho, a tax collector small in stature shimmied his way up a sycamore tree to see Jesus. Zacchaeus was longing for just a peek at Jesus and received something more than expected when Jesus picked him out of the crowd and invited himself over: "Zacchaeus, hurry and come down, for I must stay at your house today" (Luke 19:5).

Jesus sees. And he calls out. Zacchaeus was a sinner and a chief tax collector, despised among his people, and still Jesus bestowed the great honor on Zacchaeus of being his host. The Bible says that Zacchaeus, with haste, came down the tree and received Jesus joyfully. How his heart must have broken open with shards of gratitude as the man he thought he would get just a passing look at invited himself over. The crowd and religious leaders witnessed this invitation and grumbled. How could Jesus, the proclaimed Son of God, mingle with a man they abhorred? But this was Jesus' signature move: to notice the marginalized, the hated, the broken, and to bestow dignity. To move toward them in the name of love and rescue. To come into their homes and partake in the intimate act of sharing a meal.

There are people in this world who are hoping that we will make a place for ourselves at their table. We are surrounded by the disparaged, the lonely, the looked down on, and we have the opportunity, instead of walking past them, to see them and call out to them. We do not have to complicate our outreach. We can simply offer up ourselves, just like Jesus did. Jesus did not mess around with lavish dinner parties or scheduling large events. He just gave of himself. Fully. And it changed the world.

When Jesus entered homes, the brokenhearted were comforted. The shamed were cloaked in grace. The hardhearted received truth. The weary found wild doses of peace and freedom. When Jesus made a place for himself in Zacchaeus's home, it changed the man's life.

It was such an unexpected outcome. Initially, the crowd sat back with their whispered disaprovals and judgy eyes as Jesus spoke only to Zacchaeus, but it turned out the people hadn't nailed Zacchaeus's character at all. After his encounter with Jesus, Zacchaeus spoke to his Lord about all he would give to the poor. He also spoke graciously about his newfound integrity, that he would repay fourfold anyone he had defrauded. All this from an invitation. Jesus' gracious and loving act of entering into the home of a sinner resulted in this: "Today is salvation day in this home! Here he is: Zacchaeus, son of Abraham! For the Son of Man came to find and restore the lost" (Luke 19:9–10 THE MESSAGE).

This is why Jesus went into the homes of sinners: to seek and save the lost. His willingness to step into Zacchaeus's world and sit at his table resulted in a much larger work for the kingdom of God. This is what is possible when we learn the importance of being present at the table. We start with making a place for ourselves in our own homes, showing up and honoring the place God has for us every day, the place at our own table, and then that eventually leads to our eyes being opened to the powerful work of showing up and esteeming the homes of those who need healing and comfort. God will open our eyes to look up from our own lives and see all the Zacchaeuses perched in a proverbial tree, looking down and longing for a little fellowship. But to get there, it is imperative we first learn to invite ourselves to our tables.

One woman in the Bible was so skilled at making a place for herself in her own home that she was, in turn, able to serve her guests with great love and compassion. Her name was Mary. In Luke 10:38–42, we see Mary and her sister, Martha, approach the arrival of Jesus at their home in two different ways. One of them takes her place at the throne of preparation and worry, and the other takes her place at the feet of her guest.

It was such an unusual situation. First, it was customary at that time for the women to prepare and cook the meal. Martha's preoccupation with getting food to the table and doing so with excellence was exactly what she believed was expected of her. But then there was Mary. Mary sat at Jesus' feet in such a way that New

Testament scholars have noted her posture as one that exuded a desire to learn, to fully engage with what her guest brought to the table.[2]

Mary was debunking all kinds of societal norms. Surely all her life she had been taught that her place was in the kitchen, especially if guests were arriving. But when Jesus gently rebuked Martha for being frazzled with her sister's lack of help, he revealed to her, "Mary has chosen the good portion" (Luke 10:42). This use of the word *portion* can be traced back to the Psalms: "The LORD is my chosen portion and my cup; you hold my lot" (Psalm 16:5). In a situation that was probably high stress (preparing food and the home for Jesus' visit), Mary discerned what was most important. She chose the living, beating heart right in front of her. She chose Jesus. She knew exactly where she needed to invite herself—to his feet.

We can walk in the art of inviting ourselves to the feet of our guests when we become laser focused on what our portion is. Our portion is Jesus, and we never have to guess what is important to Jesus. He will always choose people. With her actions Mary stated, "If Jesus is invited into my home, then I am invited to sit at his feet. I am invited into the heart of my guests." We invite ourselves to people, not places.

Do you know where your place is in your home? According to Jesus, it's never a room; it's always a person. We don't know a lot about Mary, but I believe she must have known how to give herself a lot of grace and how to rest in the fullness of the peace that inevitably follows grace. She was so calmly secure in her place at Jesus' feet, even while her sister bustled about and scolded her for what she perceived to be laziness or a shirking of responsibilities. Mary must have been clear about how God saw her, regardless of how others saw her, thus allowing her to love herself truly and, in turn, to love and connect with her guest just as truly.

About two years into our marriage, Jeremy and I had some friends over. I loved these friends. I enjoyed them, and I was excited about the opportunity to serve them a meal. I had gradually fallen in love with cooking and gone from experimenting with the not-quite-so-appetizing onion casserole to being proficient in making an assortment of weeknight meals. The kitchen had become my art den. I was excited to now turn this new love into a gift for my friends.

Jeremy came into the kitchen that night as I was mashing the potatoes and simultaneously checking on the chicken while also somehow beginning to chop the garlic. He put his arms on my shoulders and asked if he could help. I'm sure he was just looking for a simple task to complete, such as unloading the dishes. How naïve of him! Instead, I practically barked something like, "Where have you been?! I need the trash to go out and the dinner table set and the windows opened!"

He stepped back, shocked, and said something I'll never forget: "I thought you liked cooking and having people over for dinner."

My fiery eyes darted at him, and I opened my mouth to begin my most passionate exposition on how much I loved cooking and having guests over, but nothing came out. His point was completely valid. If I really did enjoy cooking and having people over, why was I so stressed and overwhelmed? Why had I been fretting over the meal all day? Was it that I didn't want to invite myself to the table as much as I wanted to invite my Instagram-worthy food?

Feeding your people delicious food is not inherently wrong. Having a home that is welcoming and enjoyable and open to guests is good. But if all the effort it takes to reach your standards of perfection is keeping you from coming to the table, from engaging with your guests, then you've lost sight of the main goal. The goal, after all, is not to be enjoyed but to enjoy. Enjoy the people at your table. Enjoy their presence and their beating hearts and the stories they share. They are not puppets to praise you; they are urgent appointments with the heart of God. If your table is the destination for people, then the people who sit around it are a divine invitation. And you'll miss that divine invitation if all your preparation doesn't lead to you actually sitting down with them and participating in the fellowship of the table.

Thankfully, God is a redeemer. A few years later we had new friends over. Do not even get me started on hosting new friends. It's all the anxieties of first impressions and "Will we like each other?" and "Do we like eating the same thing?" We hadn't started out planning on hosting dinner, but that night as Jeremy and I were inviting ourselves to our own table, we realized, because we showed up, that we should see if our new neighbors wanted to show up too. Jeremy went over and invited them, and I planned to make dinner as everyone mingled. But that never happened.

They arrived right away, and we started talking. I kept looking at the clock and thinking, *I should get dinner on now . . . hmmm . . . actually, maybe just five more minutes of talking*. After two hours, the sun had set, and we were full on laughter and new conversation but empty of food. So Jeremy picked up the phone and ordered takeout. I could hardly believe I chose people over preparation. I invited myself to my own table and then chose my portion—and my portion was my guests. My guests showed me more of Jesus. And Jesus gave us takeout. Amen.

As we practice the art of making a place for ourselves at our own table, of giving ourselves grace and steadying our hearts in

**TIP:** To accept grace and receive an invitation for yourself to come to the table, fully present with hands open, set your phone alarm for 5:00 p.m. every day. Allow it to be a reminder to stop and say a quick prayer for the remainder of the day.

the fierce love of the One who gave up everything for us, then that peace of God that settles over our hearts becomes contagious to all who gather with us. If we do the slow and refining work of realigning ourselves with the Father's perspective, then I think we, like Mary, will find our place and come to complete peace in our own skin, at our own table. Our lens will shift and click into clarity. The meal and the tablescape will be but a blurry image on the periphery, and showing up to connect with the living, beating, image-bearer-of-God heart right in front of us will become the most important thing, the fulfillment of God's purpose for our tables.

## PRAYER FOR THE TABLE

*Lord, thank you for enjoying us. Thank you for loving us and desiring so strongly to walk with us every day. Thank you for sharing so many meals with us when you were here on this earth. Give us the grace to routinely set a place for ourselves at the table. Give us the joy to come to the table every evening with the family you placed in our homes. Change our hearts to be bearers of peace, love, and patience, not just bearers of a meal when we come to the table.*

## QUESTIONS FOR THE TABLE

1. Have you ever struggled with showing up at the table?
2. What are some of the obstacles keeping you from coming to the table every evening?
3. What are some creative or new ways that you can overcome these obstacles to start coming to the table with your family?
4. Have you entered a home and been treated the way Jesus

was treated by Mary? (To read the full story, check out Luke 10:38–42.)

5. How can you treat others the way Mary treated Jesus?

## RECIPE FOR THE TABLE

## CHEESY FONTINA DIP

**Serves 5 to 6.**

*This dish is easy and creative. It is ooey-gooey cheese baked in the oven and then served with loads of fruits and vegetables. When you're short on time and looking to simplify so you can be more intentional about bringing hope, love, peace—and your actual self—to the table, try this quick, fun dish that has the added perk of being interactive!*

## Ingredients:
1 1/2 pounds Fontina cheese, cut into 1-inch cubes
1/4 cup olive oil
3 garlic cloves, thinly sliced
1 tablespoon minced fresh thyme leaves
1 teaspoon minced fresh rosemary
1 teaspoon kosher salt
1 teaspoon freshly ground black pepper
Carrots, green apples, cauliflower, broccoli, or other veggies for
    dipping

## Instructions:
Preheat the broiler, and position the oven rack 5 inches from the heat.

Add the cubes of Fontina to a cast-iron pan. Drizzle the olive oil over the cheese.

Combine the garlic, thyme, rosemary, salt, and pepper, and sprinkle the mixture over the cheese and olive oil.

Place the pan under the broiler for 6 minutes, until the cheese is melted and bubbling and starts to brown.

Serve the cheese family-style right out of the oven in the cast-iron pan (make sure to place a hot pad over the handle so no one gets burned!). Place the fruit and veggies on a tray that is easily accessible to your guests.

NOTE: You will want to eat this right out of the oven so the cheese does not harden. I usually wait until all the guests arrive and then pop it in the oven. If the cheese does harden, just place it back under the broiler until it's melty again.

## TRICK

If a recipe calls for fresh herbs but you don't have any on hand, you can use dried. They are much more potent than fresh herbs, though, so a good rule of thumb is 1 tablespoon of fresh herbs = 1 teaspoon of dried herbs.

# *three*

# INVITING OTHERS TO THE TABLE

*"Come, everyone who thirsts, come to the waters;*
*and he who has no money, come, buy and eat!"*

ISAIAH 55:1

I'm pretty sure I learned some academically useful things in high school—probably? hopefully?—but mostly I remember learning how hard it is to live in this world. My first day of high school was dramatically horrific. I don't remember the classes I went to or the homework I was assigned. I don't even remember experiencing the stereotypical high school situation with my locker not opening. I only have one vivid memory of that day: lunch time.

That first day, I was not only starting out at a new school but also entering a new school district. So I had zero friends from middle school to undergo the transition with me. I remember walking into the cafeteria, trying to figure out how I was going to make instant friends. I was painfully shy in high school, so, actually, the prospect of instant friends was out of the realm of possibility.

I calmly marched to the back of the room and found what I thought was an empty table. We did not have cell phones back then, so I had nothing to distract me or to make me look busy except the careful and calculated way I peeled my orange. I repeated to myself all the things brave little girls say: *This is only the first day. You are in a new district. You will make friends.* But my triumphant speech was interrupted by an annoyed voice saying, "Excuse me. You're at our table."

There must have been a hundred tables in that cafeteria, but because my luck is spectacular, I had ended up sitting at the one and only cool kids' table. I turned bright red and scooted my orange peels into my brown bag before quickly removing myself. I had been swiftly and promptly uninvited.

Being uninvited has to be one of the worst feelings in the history of feelings. My encouraging little-girl speech was replaced with self-directed harshness: *They are better than you, they are older, they are prettier, they are smarter . . .* You might find it strange that I remember this story from such a long time ago, and perhaps you're hoping I will see a therapist someday soon. But here's why I hold on to this story: if being uninvited made me feel all those unlovely things back then, I want to consciously remember today what being invited can communicate to a soul.

Jesus was and is the ultimate inviter. He has a table. He calls us to it. May we follow suit and use the table he has given us to reflect his table. May we fling open our doors when we hear a knock. May we serve what we have with joy and gratitude. May we understand that a lot of days there are people walking around replaying a harsh reckoning of themselves and their own failings, and may we interrupt that with an invitation. May we replace their internal dialogue with, "You are loved. You are known. You are seen. Come with me, and eat!"

Even though inviting is one of the most powerful displays of

God's love, even though I have experienced the power of being invited, it's still hard for me to invite others to our table. It's hard because at my core I am afraid no one will show up. But guess who else had a banquet to which no one showed up?

In Luke 14:15, Jesus told a parable of a great banquet. A parable of a man who prepared a great feast and invited a lot of guests. When it was time for the banquet to begin, the excuses from those he'd invited started to roll in. One had to tend to his field, another had just gotten married, and another was busy taking care of his animals. Has this ever happened to you? It's certainly happened to me once or twice. I invited but few ended up at my table. How did I respond? I did a lot of things. After my guests left I sulked. Then I judged the people who didn't show up, and then I judged the attractiveness of my home and the deliciousness of my food. But, according to this parable, there is only one thing we need to do in response to absent guests: go out and find other guests!

If you have ten servings of stew and only four guests, go find six other guests! Just start sending out texts to nearby friends or knocking on the doors of neighbors. Here's the thing: They might already be busy. They might not come. But what if they aren't busy? What if at that exact moment they were starting to deflate under the weight of their day? And what if your invitation could be the hope that slams into their desperation?

After one year—and I mean exactly 365 days—of marriage, Jeremy got on a plane and flew to another land for a deployment for six months. This was hard on me. The mornings were okay. I'd wake up and think, *Okay, the countdown has shortened by one day! Look at me, I am doing this thing. I am living in a different state with no family and without my husband and doing this life God has called me to.* But, as the evenings drew near, I would unravel. I would miss Jeremy coming through the door at the end of the day. I became painfully aware of how quiet my home was. Many nights I sat at my dining room table and sobbed. I called it the table of tears.

The thing about being a military wife is, you have to become really okay and really comfortable with asking for things. Like asking for help. Asking for friendship. Asking for prayer. Asking to go out with your friend and her husband even though it's their date night. This was my first deployment, and I was really bad at asking for help. I was really bad at inviting myself. Then, one night, just as I was sitting down to my usual meal of tears and heartache, I got a text from a friend: "Hey, do you want to come over and have dinner with our family? I made an abundance of food."

I could not text back quickly enough. I went to my friend's house. I ate. I shared how hard this deployment had been. They prayed for me. I read bedtime stories to their boys. I left happy and invited. All of this from just a text. All of this from an invitation to come and eat! And do you know what? I do not remember what we ate. I only remember that there was a place for me at the table and an invitation to come eat.

Right before Jeremy and I started coming consistently to the table together, we volunteered our home to be a meeting place for a Bible study. The leader of the group called us a few days later and told us there were fifteen people signed up, mostly couples. I was both excited and a little horrified. We did not have one room that could fit fifteen people comfortably. But we did have an upstairs loft that we were using mostly for storage, so we decided to reinvent the area.

After one long Sunday and lots of shopping through our own home (as my friend Myquillyn taught me, we don't have to go out and buy new things for our spaces; we can go through our own home and find things we already have and repurpose them), we had taken a dim storage area and turned it into a welcoming meeting area. We turned an awkward corner into a tea and coffee station. We placed a fun pub table near the entrance for snacks. We found enough chairs and arranged them in a funky circle to facilitate conversation. It quickly became one of my favorite and quickest renovations.

The night of our first meeting I arranged a bounty of snacks on our pub table and made sure we had enough tea and coffee to feed a platoon of soldiers. Then the guests started to arrive. All. **THREE**. Guests. We then discovered that exactly zero of our three guests liked coffee or tea. Two of them could not even think of eating because they were full on dinner, and the third was allergic to just about everything I had on my table.

For two months, our misfit group met in our loft at 7:30 p.m. every Tuesday. Rather than growing, though, our group went from five to four, and to be clear, Jeremy and I were two of the four. Our pub table started to fill with dust instead of dishes. The saddest part is, even though we were reading the Bible together each week, what we knew about one another could be boiled down to our favorite weather and our allergies. Jeremy and I were a little dismayed and a lot heartbroken. This was our first time hosting in our new home. I had been sure our house would be brimming with masses of people, intelligent conversation, and delicious food. I could not have been more wrong. I never would have guessed this was what God had in store.

Sometimes we invite the world to our tables and only one neighbor shows up. But we know how Jesus feels about the one— he'll leave the whole flock for just one. He'll serve up a whole feast for just one. He would have died for just one. So though it may feel discouraging and a little like our efforts aren't being put to the utmost use, we need to remember Jesus' heart toward the one. As we practice this art of adoring, serving, and delighting in the one

God has placed right in front of us, we will begin to believe that all our efforts are for his glory and can expertly be used by him.

With all this in mind, Jeremy and I started to pray about what we should be doing. Even though the study in our home looked different than we had expected, it was important that we still showed up for the two guests as much as we would have shown up for the fifteen. As we prayed I felt Jesus encourage me, *Be faithful with little.* He nudged us to start inviting our study to the dinner table.

At first, this seemed difficult to pull off. The leader of the study had defined the terms of our group meetings early on. Study started at 7:30 p.m., and we were only to provide light snacks. We did not want to disrespect his decisions or his leadership. But as Jesus spoke to our hearts about investing more into this small community, we decided we'd show up to what God was leading us to do and suggest a change. I e-mailed both the leader and the lone other gentleman still showing up and asked if we could move our study up to 7:00 p.m. and if we could also invite them over for a meal rather than light snacks. They did not have to bring anything. Nothing. Just themselves. I'd have a home-cooked meal prepared for us to eat, and we could do the study at the table. When I opened their e-mails in response, I sat shocked at their agreement. It was so easy. It was so simple. Come and eat? They said yes. Jeremy and I were about to learn the ministry of a meal.

Over the next several weeks of our study, we learned more about one another than we had during the previous three months. The only thing that had changed was the location of our gathering. We went from the loft to the table. The invitation was now clearly "come and eat."

On our second night of trying this new format, Jim, the other faithful part of our study, spoke up. "I'm really grateful for this home-cooked meal. I've been eating out a lot lately. My wife left me, and we are in the middle of a divorce I don't want."

This statement alarmed me to no end. It was not so much that Jim was going through this heartbreaking situation but that we had not been able to walk with him through it for the past three months we had been meeting. But then we served him a meal, and he returned the favor. He gave us his heart.

Jim finished sharing his whole story, and our tiny community rose to the occasion. We asked questions and went into prayer with fervor, each of us pleading with God and thanking God. It was a holy moment. And it all happened right there at the table. For the next two months, I kept showing up with food, and the two guys kept showing up with stories.

At one meeting our leader spoke up about why his wife was not attending the study. For nearly ten years they had tried to get pregnant. There had been hopeful years and gut-wrenching years. There had been mountains of doubt that only seemed to lead into valleys with hardly ever a summit in sight. But, finally, she had gotten pregnant and was now almost due. Extremely tired, she was staying at home to rest and have some time to herself on the nights of our study.

Of course, we had all speculated about why his wife was not there, but we never could have guessed the real reason. If ever there was a time in my life when a veil was dropping from my eyes, it was during that study. How was it that we'd sat in a circle reading the Bible together for months on end and only been able to have lofty discourse *about* Jesus' life on earth but not conversation detailing Jesus in our very own lives? In our living, our suffering, our rejoicing. Jesus is not to be just talked about; he is to be lived out.

For weeks after that, we asked thoughtful questions in between eager bites. We moved slowly through the meal because we knew we were actually moving through our hearts. Heartaches. Answered prayers. Jeremy and I were hooked; we loved taking part in the table as a holy place God uses to radically engage his people.

Two years later, we signed up to host Bible study in our home again. This time we also signed up to lead. When the pastor asked if there were any specifications we wanted to include about our study, we had just one: we wanted it to take place at the table while sharing a meal together. Our new group started with a handful of couples. After a few weeks, word got out about our meals, and other people started joining. We eventually had to close the group for the sheer reason that we couldn't fit anymore people in our home. We also had to split the group, and, thankfully, another couple stepped up to start hosting in their home.

One evening, as we were gathering around the table, bubbling over with gratitude for the community God had allowed us to be part of, it occurred to me that just a few years before, this table held four instead of twelve. The work he did in our hearts with our tiny group had prepared us to better love and serve the table he now seated with a whole host of people. I believe God loves to start with us in the small. He can reveal grand and imperative lessons to us in the most mundane and humble of circumstances. God is faithful. We need only to say, "Okay, this is where you have me right now. I'll keep showing up faithfully. What do you want to show me?"

Inviting others to the table ushers Jesus' life and love into our homes. I think that's why Jesus showed up to so many tables. It's why Jesus invited himself to the table of a chief tax collector and the tax collector received him so joyfully. Sharing a meal at the table naturally leads to intimacy. Eating in front of someone is, by nature, a vulnerable act. When we create a space for people to open their mouths, they just might do something more than eat. They just might open their hearts too. In many ways, the fork is the most widely used and unrecognized microphone.

The route to my friend's house is a path traced on my heart. I showed up there too many times to count while I was in college. She shouldn't have been available then. She was pregnant with her first child and then her second, but I kept showing up and she kept opening her door. It never mattered what we ate; it was a feast for my soul. She'd slice the bread, and I'd cut open my heart.

There was a lot going on in my life in those days. I'd met my soon-to-be-husband (hint: no, I hadn't). I'd changed my major two—no, three—times. My best friend's boyfriend didn't like me, so she stopped liking me too. And I worked a job with guys who threw nasty remarks and lustful looks at me and the other girls at all hours of our shifts. But I kept showing up to work. I kept showing up to church. And I kept knocking on that friend's door.

One evening I showed up not even intending to. I think I was sad, but it was too deep for me to understand it. I was broken. I was wild. She opened the door, and maybe she saw my tears first. Or my hands gripping a piece of paper. She let me in. She always did. She was nine months pregnant, probably tired, and clearly trying to get dinner on the table for her husband, but she didn't let me bear any of that. I read the letter to her, the one from a boy who told me how bad of a Christian I was. That I couldn't possibly love Jesus, because if I did I would celebrate his relationship with another friend of mine, even though it was a harmful one. Before I could finish, she floated the paper out of my hands and into hers. We went straight to her grill and lit those words on fire. Then we grilled burgers, and I ate those charred words (which tasted especially delicious with gobs of melted cheese and loads of tangy yellow mustard). A meal can break through the chords of hate and strengthen us for the journey right where we stand.

My friend would later tell me that it was so easy to have me over—that I wasn't particular about what she served me or whether her home was clean. But she didn't know that she had been saving me one meal at a time. Her table had been a safe place simply because she'd always made a place for me.

Now I am grown and have my own table, my own safe place for others.

A few years ago, I was scrutinizing my table right before a group of friends arrived for dinner. I was trying to figure out if there would be enough room at the table, enough food, if I had enough energy after a long day, but then I realized I only needed to laser focus on one thing. I walked right over to my table and stared it down. Then I took a deep breath and pointed my finger at it, proclaiming, "You're a safe place." Thankfully there was no one else in the house to witness this and decide that perhaps I was not sane enough for guests that evening, so I went on with my declaration. "You're going to carry deep gut-felt laughs and heart-wrenching sobs. You will carry whispered prayers and hands that find each other and new love and a lot of tired love. For decades, you will hold flowers and drinks and tears. You will bear messy plates and messy hearts. And people will keep coming, because you. Are. A. Safe. Place. And no matter what's going on in my life or what state of readiness you are in, I will keep inviting people to come to you." And then I walked off. Best conversation I ever had with my table. I highly recommend it.

I was learning then and am reminded today that for me, for

> **TIP:** Think of one way to practice a habit that will turn your table into a safe zone. It might be to speak less or ask more questions. Practice this one habit for a full month, and then move on to another one. You might just transform your whole table!

Jeremy, for any number of people to experience the blessing of having a safe place at the table, an invitation must come first. Before people show up to the table, we must invite them. We must get over our fear. We must look to Jesus, a master at the invitation.

Jesus never complicated the whole business of having a meal with others. Even today the invitation is as simple and clear as ever: "Look! I stand at the door and knock. If you hear my voice and open the door, I will come in, and we will share a meal together as friends" (Revelation 3:20 NLT).

We don't have to overthink or complicate our invitations before our tables can become honored as safe places. We can be moved to "Look!" as Jesus exclaims, and invite others to share a meal with us as friends. That's it. Simplify. Acknowledge the beating hearts that are on our paths, and invite them to share a meal. And when we start practicing the art of inviting, we will be carried further into the heart of Jesus. We will catch on fire, our souls blazing with God's love for the people of this world. It's undeniably difficult to hate or judge someone while you sit close and break bread together. It's nearly impossible to eat a meal with someone and not acknowledge in them the image of our God. Maybe this is why Jesus kept showing up at tables?

Are you longing to love the people God has in your life more fully? Your neighbors? Your family? Your coworkers? I longed for that. I still long for it. When we encounter the real, living, and loving God who saved our souls, how can we not want that for all people? For a long time, I made it complicated to show Jesus' love to the people in my life. I tried to arrange awkward coffee dates where I could read the Bible with a new believer, or I'd try to serve them in ways I'm not gifted. But Jesus showed me how easy and magnificent it is to love someone and reveal his love to them from a place I show up to every day: my table.

It's simple, because we are all in need of a meal. We're not offering something to someone that's not necessary. It's holy, because we are doing exactly what Jesus chose to do so many times while he was on this earth.

Who is at your table? Whom have you had to your table? We can start small with our invitations. God will meet us on the journey.

## PRAYER FOR THE TABLE

*Jesus, thank you for modeling to us how we can love others well as you walked this earth and consistently showed up to meals with others. Thank you for this daily ritual of eating that can be used by you to create community right where you have us. Grant us vision and bravery as we step out into our neighborhoods, our workplaces, and our communities and invite others over to a meal. May we be controlled by your Spirit as we step out. May we extend the invitation and trust you to do the rest.*

## QUESTIONS FOR THE TABLE

1. Share a story or a memory you have about being invited to a table during a time when you especially needed the invitation. If you don't have one, ask God to bring someone onto your path to show you the power of being invited to come and eat.
2. Is there anything holding you back from inviting people to your table? What is it, and how can you overcome it?
3. "Come and eat!" is such a simple invitation, and it's the invitation Jesus used often. Are you drawn to the simplicity of this invitation? Are there ways you complicate the invitation for your friends or family to come to the table?

## RECIPE FOR THE TABLE

## EASY, DELICIOUS BOLOGNESE SAUCE
## WITH SWEET POTATO NOODLES

**Serves 4 to 5.**

*I learned a long time ago that I'm more likely to invite people to my
table if I have some easy and delicious recipes in my arsenal that I know
turn out well every time. This recipe is one from my mom, and if I could,
I would eat it every night. I have also been known to eat spoonfuls of
this sauce before even serving it over noodles. It's that good! Make
plenty of this recipe to serve all your guests, and if you have leftovers,
this tastes amazing the next day!*

## Ingredients:

2 tablespoons olive oil

1/2 red onion, diced

1 pound ground beef, 80 percent lean

3 garlic cloves, minced

1 tablespoon dried oregano

1/4 teaspoon crushed red pepper (optional)

1 1/4 cups dry red wine (or beef stock), divided

1 (28-ounce) can crushed tomatoes

2 tablespoons tomato paste

1 tablespoon salt

1/2 teaspoon pepper

1/4 cup heavy cream

1/2 cup freshly grated Parmesan cheese

1 sweet potato, peeled and spiralized (for sweet potato noodles) or
    1 (16-ounce) package spaghetti

## Instructions:

Heat the olive oil in a large skillet over medium-high heat. Add the onion, and cook until softened, about 3 minutes.

Add the ground beef, and cook, crumbling the meat with a spatula, for 5 to 7 minutes, until it begins to brown.

Stir in the garlic, oregano, and crushed red pepper, and cook for 1 more minute.

Pour 1 cup of the wine (or beef stock) into the skillet, stirring to scrape up any browned bits.

Add the tomatoes, tomato paste, salt, and pepper, and stir until combined. Bring to a boil, reduce the heat to low, and simmer for 10 minutes, uncovered.

Add the cream and the remaining 1/4 cup wine (or beef stock) to the sauce. Simmer for 8 to 10 minutes, stirring occasionally until thickened. Turn off the heat, and stir in the Parmesan cheese.

Bring a large pot of water to a boil. Add the spiralized sweet potato noodles. Boil for 4 to 6 minutes but no longer than 6 minutes. Drain the noodles. (If using spaghetti noodles, cook them according to the package directions.)

Place the noodles on a plate, and spoon the sauce on top. Sprinkle with more Parmesan cheese if desired.

To see photos of this recipe and how to spiralize the sweet potato, visit http://oursavorylife.com/how-to-make-sweet-potato-noodles/.

## TRICK

The best way to get rid of stuck-on browned pieces of meat from your pan is through deglazing, which will also create a richer sauce. Just *slowly* pour in the amount of liquid the recipe calls for (wine or broth work well), and use a wooden spatula to quickly scrape up browned bits as the liquid hits the pan. The trick here is to pour the liquid in slowly, not all at once.

*four*

# A VISION FOR THE TABLE

*Jesus didn't run projects, establish ministries,*
*or put on events. He ate meals.*

—TIM CHESTER, *A MEAL WITH JESUS*

For a long time, I sat in awe of everything that was starting to happen around my table. I'd walk away after a meal and think, *Wow! That was amazing. That story. That way our guest loved on me even though I'd intended to love on her. That celebration. That prayer.* I was in awe of the power of what God can do over a meal. But then it occurred to Jeremy and me that, despite our best intentions, we were simply letting it all happen *to us*, and there could be so much more if we intentionally partnered with God and his work by creating a vision for our table. This helped us shift from reacting to purposefully implementing what we wanted to foster.

A specific vision for the table can seem a little extravagant, right? As I journeyed down this path my first thought was, *Well, then do I need a vision for the guest room? The kitchen? The bathroom?!* But as I continued it occurred to me that the table is the place Jesus consistently used to further his ministry and display his love. It's the one item we all have, and it's the one place God invites us to every evening. The most powerful place God can use us is usually the exact place he already has us. I used to think that God wanted to send me to Africa or Thailand to be used as a mighty force in his hand. I prayed and waited for the call to go, but it never came. I eventually realized there was one place God kept sending me, and every day at that. He'd always send me to my dining room table for a meal.

Barbara Kingsolver once wrote, "If I had to quantify it, I'd say 75 percent of my crucial parenting effort has taken place during or surrounding the time our family convenes for our evening meal."[1] Could you imagine if Barbara and her family were not showing up at the table? As I often say, I believe everyone has at least one life-defining moment that happens at a table—and probably many more—but we won't experience those powerful moments if we're not showing up in the first place. If we can bring purpose and focus to our time at the table, God will use us powerfully not just in our own homes but also in the world. Before the call to go to Africa, perhaps there is just the call to keep showing up at our table?

Identifying a strong and simple vision can help us funnel all our actions through our main goal. If what we're thinking about doing doesn't align with our vision, then we shouldn't proceed. According to Laurie Beth Jones, author of *The Path,* a good vision should be

1. no more than a single sentence long
2. easily understood by a twelve-year-old
3. able to be recited by memory at gunpoint[2]

Similarly, a potent vision for the table is one that relies heavily on the power of God. It keeps us humble. It reminds us that we can only set out to do the work of God by the power and guidance of God. It helps us to remain laser focused.

Jeremy and I talked a lot about our vision for the table. In the beginning, we hadn't yet learned what makes a more effective vision, and we weren't quite as focused. I kept coming up with elaborate and visual statements, and Jeremy had to keep reminding me to be simple. I was hoping my vision for the table could somehow include four-course dinners and a drink menu. Plus, we needed to work in the ever-popular yet totally unplanned dance party. And themed nights. I wanted our vision for the table to somehow include every possible outcome of a meal in our home. And you better believe I know how to throw a themed dinner party.

But Jeremy kept challenging me to get smaller and simpler with my grand vision. So we started praying and asking God to show us some consistent themes we'd been seeing at our table. We noted that we were constantly hosting new people in our home because we move a lot, we had welcomed a lot of hurting people to our table, and we were also consistently bringing people who do not know Jesus to our table. What could God want to ultimately use us for at our table when this is what and who he kept inviting?

Casting a vision for your table does not have to be complicated. You can come on this journey alongside me. What is it that God has placed on your heart about the specific way he works through the gatherings at your table? Are there specific people that keep showing up? Specific needs that continuously arise or are met at your table? Taking a deeper look at what God is already doing at your table can illuminate the path to a vision. Also, if you have a vision or mission for your life, or even a life verse, look at that, because it is probably going to closely tie into the ministry of your table. Do you have a passion for the homeless? For saving money? For your community? Most likely your vision will have an aspect of that passion.

When we come to God seeking him to help give the time at our tables purpose, we are able to partner with him to bring his love into our homes and communities daily. What I love about creating a personal vision for our tables is that my vision will look different from yours. God has given each of us different passions and different gifts to carry out his will. We need to stay true to how God wants to uniquely use us at our own tables instead of trying to copy what we might see others doing. I'll show you how this exercise worked for me in hopes that it will jump-start your own journey.

First, I wrote down a verse that has carried me through much of my life thus far. This verse has shown up when I've needed to decide how to act in a certain situation or when I've needed to know what God is calling me to do. Even though I haven't officially declared this my life verse, I have found that I always come back to it: "By this everyone will know that you are my disciples, if you love one another" (John 13:35 NIV).

Once I had my verse written out, I leaned into why God illuminated this verse in my life. As I considered this and prayed, I found that loving others in a way that people know I belong to Jesus is something I desperately desire to demonstrate at the table, and as I have started to remind myself of this, I have found the freedom to let go of things I struggle with that don't align with this verse, like judgment or disgust or fear—all things that shut down dialogue at a table. Instead, keeping my focus on my verse allows me to consistently choose to funnel all my actions and reactions at the table through the lens of loving so extravagantly that it can only point back to Jesus.

Take a moment to write out a verse that has been consistent in your life. Look into the freedom your verse gives you when you bring it to the table. Freedom to be fully yourself instead of trying to be someone else? Freedom to pay more attention to the people at the table instead of what food you can bring to the table? Freedom to invite people from all different backgrounds to the table?

We can find powerful visions for the life of God's chosen people in the Bible. Nehemiah used his life to rebuild the wall in Jerusalem so the people would return to God. Joshua led the people of Israel into the promised land so God's promises would be fulfilled. Mary birthed and mothered Jesus so he could enter this world and save humanity. One consistent thing we see in all effective visions is that they include an action and a positive outcome of that action.

I once heard a pastor say that he and his wife's goal for their table was to make it a deep breath for all the people who came to it, so their guests could experience the rest of God. What action do you want to take at your table, and what outcome do you want to see as a result? Note that the outcomes for many of the people in the Bible were not immediate. For many of them it took a lifetime of doing the action before the outcome came to full fruition. But it was the steady and persistent work they leaned into with a clear vision that allowed them to keep working despite setbacks or discouragement.

This journey God wants to take you on might be one of a lifetime, so do not let that hinder you as you write out your vision. So far, we each have a verse that God has laid on our hearts and are standing at the beginning of the journey God has given us to live out at our tables, which will also eventually overflow into other areas of our lives. The next step is to identify the outcome we desire.

Return to your piece of paper and draw two columns right below your verse. Title the first column "action" and the second column "outcomes." Fill these columns with what actions you want to take at your table and the outcomes you want them to produce. My first column was filled with actions like "feed," "listen," "love," "pray for," and "show compassion to," and my second column was filled with outcomes like "to be filled," "to feel heard," "to know the love of Jesus," "to experience the peace of God," and "to open the door to God's generosity." The outcome is what you want people to come away with because of what you put into action at your table.

| ACTIONS | OUTCOMES |
| --- | --- |
| Feed | To be filled emotionally, spiritually, physically |
| Listen | To feel rested and heard |
| (Love) | To know the (love) of Jesus |
| Pray for | To experience the peace of God |
| Show compassion to | To open the door to God's generosity |

Once you have written out your verse and a list of actions and outcomes, circle consistent themes emerging in the columns and the verse. This will bring focus. For me, the theme jumped out:

"By this everyone will know that you are my disciples, if you (love) one another" (John 13:35 NIV).

The word *love* appeared in my verse and in both of my columns. Coupled with the issues God was laying on my heart, I knew that my main purpose at my table was to show extravagant love, love despite a broken and hurting world, love that could only point to Jesus.

Now we get to write out our full vision. I am a big fan of writing without editing and then circling back to simplify. I do this in almost every area of writing (even my grocery list—three bags of chips? Probably just need one!). Your vision can be long and include all the verbs and adjectives your heart desires, but make sure it lines up with the theme you just identified. Mine followed suit:

> Inviting others to the table to share a delicious meal, so they can share their hearts and we can love them well and encourage them and pray for them. So they will get curious about this big love and ask why, giving us the opportunity to share the gospel. And then they will be in our lives FOREVER!

As you can see, I got a little carried away. And just a tad clingy. But now we get to simplify. Once you have everything written down, grab a red pen and start eliminating. We want the simplest, most memorable vision statement and one that stays consistent with the theme we already identified. This is what mine looked like:

> ~~Inviting others to the table to share a delicious meal, so they can share their hearts and~~ we can love them well ~~and encourage them and pray for them~~. So they will ~~get curious about this big love and~~ ask why—**giving us the opportunity to share the gospel.** ~~And then they will be in our lives FOREVER!~~

At the heart of our vision, once I edited and cleared away the excess, was a desire to love so well at the table that our guests will get curious and open a discussion about this love, hopefully giving us an opportunity to point them to Jesus. But even this was a bit of a clunky statement. One night as we were lying in bed, talking about this vision, Jeremy pushed me to simplify even further. He kept saying, "But why do you want to love extravagantly?" And I'd unleash a list of reasons why. But he kept pushing me to get more narrow, which, to be honest, was annoying me so much that finally in exasperation I spat out that I wanted to love people so well that "they'll ask why!"

Jeremy, calm as usual, responded, "Great! Our vision is: **To love so extravagantly, they'll ask why!**"

On the surface, it seems simple, but so much can overflow out of the goal of loving extravagantly. It can mean praying, it can mean listening, it can mean serving a delicious meal. For us, loving extravagantly means that we purposefully lean into God for guidance with each guest we have in our home. We might have a guest who is going through a hard time or a guest who has not had a home-cooked meal in weeks or a guest who wants to celebrate a new job. Whatever it is, we look to Jesus so he can show us what it looks like to extravagantly love that person. All so that person will experience the irresistible love of Jesus and ask us what this love is that they are receiving.

> **TIP:** Think of your vision for the table in terms of an elevator speech. Can you recite it in the time it takes for people to go from one floor to another in an elevator?

As Jeremy and I talked about our purpose, we dreamed about all God could do through us if we put our hearts and hands to this work of loving lavishly at the table, without hindrance even through trials or discouragement. We want to trust what Jesus calls us to do at the table in the hope that it will affect the hurting world outside our doors. We are convinced that if we can continue to strive more fully toward this boundless love, then people will be lining up to hear about the love of Jesus. We want God to use us to change our neighborhood, and then our community, and then maybe our whole city.

It's important to bring everyone under your roof into agreement with this vision: your spouse or roommates or children. Jeremy and I took our time with our vision. We talked about it at the table often. It took weeks for us to land on a vision that was simple, one we could memorize, and one that embodied our desire for our table. We even declared a vision, but then, as we dug deeper and realized we'd missed the point, we reassessed. There's no strict deadline on completing your vision. This journey is an exciting one. Feel free to get creative, using markers or notecards. It's a great time of journeying with the people in your home and with God into the heart of how he wants to use you right in your very own home.

Jeremy and I wrote out our vision, framed it, and put it on a wall in our kitchen. It is ever before us. Our prayer at the table has now also become spectacularly simple: "Jesus, please bring people to our table so we can love them so extravagantly they'll ask why." Our table hasn't looked the same since.

## PRAYER FOR THE TABLE

*Father, thank you for choosing us to pour out your love into the world. Thank you for giving us a common way to show and practice and accept your love: inviting others to come and eat. Grant us a vision for what you want to see happen around our table. Illuminate the specific gifts you have given me and the needs you want to meet at my table so that I and the people under this roof can partner with you to fulfill your will.*

## QUESTIONS FOR THE TABLE

1. Do you have a life verse or current mission statement?
2. What specific kinds of people are most often at your table or what specific needs do you see consistently met at your table?

3. Grab a piece of paper, write out your verse, and fill out two columns of actions and outcomes you want to see happen at your table. What themes do you see presented in the columns and verse?

4. As a family, write out a vision. Remember that you can start out with a longer statement and then simplify.

**BONUS:** Once you've written your vision, go to your table the next night with some pens or crayons or paint and write your vision on a large piece of paper. Then hang it in a place where you all can see it!

## RECIPE FOR THE TABLE

## BALSAMIC GLAZED PORK

Serves 5 to 6.

*This recipe is a quick, no-fuss meal with lots of options for serving, so you can focus less on the food and enjoy more time with your people as you gather to discover a vision for your table!*

## Ingredients:

1 (2- to 3-pound) boneless pork tenderloin, fat trimmed

1/4 teaspoon salt

1/4 teaspoon pepper

1 cup chicken or vegetable broth

1/2 cup balsamic vinegar

2 tablespoons apple cider vinegar

1 tablespoon honey

3 garlic cloves, smashed

1 yellow onion, quartered

1 1/2 cups basmati rice
Oil for cooking eggs
5 to 6 eggs (or 1 egg per person)

## Instructions:

Rub the pork all over with salt and pepper.

In a small bowl mix together the broth, balsamic vinegar, apple cider vinegar, and honey.

Place the pork in a slow cooker, and pour the liquid all over the pork. Place the garlic and onion around the pork.

Cook on low for 6 to 8 hours or on high for 4 hours. The meat should easily shred with two forks.

When the pork is finished, let it rest, and cook the basmati rice according to the package instructions.

Place a large, nonstick skillet over medium heat. Add the oil, and when the oil is hot, crack a few eggs into the pan. (My pan holds three eggs at a time.) Allow the eggs to cook for about 1 minute. Reduce the heat to low, cover with a lid, and allow the eggs to cook for an additional 2 minutes. The eggs are done (over-easy) when a white film has formed over top of the eggs, but the yolk is still liquidy.

To serve, remove the pork from the slow cooker and shred with two forks. Spoon some basmati rice onto a plate. Top with balsamic pork, and be sure to get some of the juices and onions onto the rice. Top with the over-easy egg.

ADDITIONAL SERVING OPTIONS: You can also serve the shredded pork on top of baked sweet potatoes (cooked in the oven at 400 degrees for 40 minutes). Or serve the pork on hamburger buns with sweet potato fries.

TRICK ————————————————————————————————

Unlike a chuck roast, when cooking large cuts of pork, like a pork shoulder or pork butt, you want to remove the excess fat. If it is not removed, it will cook down and create a very greasy and oily sauce. Be sure to take a sharp knife and remove any white fatty parts of pork before cooking.

# *five*

# BROKENNESS AT THE TABLE

*"Can God spread a table in the wilderness?"*

PSALM 78:19

There is a table I never want to return to, and it's also a table I'll never forget. It's the bar top I sat at around midnight in the red-light district of Thailand when I was twenty-three. I was there working with a ministry that rescues women from prostitution. Before I stepped up to that bar top, the solution to this international problem had seemed so simple: tell these women they did not have to sleep with strange men every night or give up their valuable bodies for money. I was coming as a brave white knight to help them understand this simple, life-changing truth. They would rejoice. They would come away with us. We'd shut down the whole prostitution ring in Bangkok, Thailand.

But after a few minutes of sitting at that dark, open-air bar,

I started to see how mistaken I was, how incredibly intricate the whole system is. Most of the girls I spoke to had been taken from their villages up north and were ten or more hours away from any family. The pimps had gone into remote and poor villages and promised parents they would take their daughters to the big city of Bangkok and get them a good education. They had offered hope amidst a desperate and bleak situation, and so the parents gave their daughters to these pimps in hopes that they could break the cycle of poverty. Of course, once the girls arrived in Bangkok, they were faced with the reality of what life was to be from there on out. They were now owned, and their bodies would be sold every night to pay the piper.

That first night at the bar table, I was calm. My heart felt like the slow, low tide of the ocean transfixed by the moon. Freedom seemed tangible and thick from where I sat, but three feet in front of me, where the women tended the bar, there might as well have been metal barriers, a cage these women were condemned to. I sat sickened with the brokenness of it all, feeling incredibly small against the weight of evil. And the men all around me sat like gods.

I watched each man step up to the bar, slide over some cash, point at a woman, and then leave with her by his side. Seeing these women who were fearfully and wonderfully made, not to mention deeply loved by God, being pointed at and surrendered into buyers' arms nearly paralyzed me with grief. My dismal and swift fall into despair was interrupted when one of the Thai women behind the bar, intrigued by my presence, asked, "You a pretty little blond girl. What you want?"

"I'll take a Diet Coke, please." I stretched out the word *please* like I was stretching out a bridge. One I wanted her to cross, to travel on to the other side of the bar so she could leave with me. In my mind this bridge only needed to be three feet long. In reality it needed to be the sturdiest, longest, safest bridge anyone could build. One does not simply take three steps out of evil.

She handed me a glass, and I wrapped my hands around it like it was an anchor. I began talking. The thing about asking someone a question, especially someone you don't know, is that it can feel like you are lifting a large boulder. What is underneath? A scorpion that will attack? A snake that will slither away? A crippled plant longing for the sun? I lifted the boulder with my careful words, and I hoped to find a beating heart that said, "I'm grateful you came to my table. Please stay awhile."

My first question to her came from shock. Shock that girls did not run away from this slavery. It was abrupt, and my face grew red and hot as the question dripped from my lips. "Why are you here?"

The girl explained she'd had great hopes of running away and finding a path back to her family, but the pimp had convinced her that her family needed this good money she was making, reminding her that her family back home was starving. So she, like many of the other girls, stayed for the survival of her family and sent most of her earnings back home every week. This system was bigger than I could have fathomed.

Every night for one week, my team of girls and I would arrive at a new bar top and talk with the women working there. I learned about the evil of the world at those tables. I learned that the cost of sex with a Thai woman is twenty American dollars. I talked to men from all over the world who would sit at those same tables with me, their bodies aching for a little pleasure, my whole being aching for a lot of justice. I wondered at how loudly our desires clashed against each other in the space between us. At this table I learned that in this world, money can buy you what it shouldn't even be able to touch.

The ministry I was with took a very long-suffering approach to rescuing women out of prostitution. They had to. The wounds were too deep, the destruction so absolute. The strategy every night was for us to buy a woman and take her out to dinner, to establish a relationship. It was to give her a reprieve from the night. We would feed her stomach and ultimately offer food for her soul. We'd take her from that rotting bar table and sit with her at a table marked with hope.

At dinner, we would share about the free English-speaking school we ran during the day. This always caught the women's attention, because a Thai woman who can speak English makes more money simply because more men want to buy a woman they can understand. At the class the ministry would teach English but also always end with prayer and the gospel story. Over time, they shared with the women that they also had a school that trained them to do hair and nails and to sew and that this would make as much money, if not more, than their jobs as prostitutes. Gradually, women were able to leave prostitution and enter another profession through this ministry. We met many of these women. A rescued woman is a glorious thing to behold.

Those initial bar tables, though, where it all began, were hard tables to sit at. They weren't filled with family friends. They didn't brim over with laughter and gooey casseroles. The conversations were always raw and hard. We never ended with dessert and coffee. We never left the table feeling full and satisfied. I always felt helpless and startled. These tables were splintered and worn. They were soaked in strong alcohol and cheap cologne. They held the stories of a thousand sins.

I sat at those tables for one week. I placed my hand on the bar and ordered my drink. I shook the hands of women who were inherently worth more than they could have ever dreamed. I started the process of opening a door that revealed a Rescuer more loving, more powerful, and more gentle than they could ever hope to find in a man—someone who wouldn't just call them beautiful and speak the American names their pimps gave them, but a Man who would call them clean and pure, who knew their Thai names, even though his favorite name for them is Beloved.

On my last night in Thailand, I sat at a new wooden bar table and ordered my usual Diet Coke. I fumbled to find the drink, to wrap my fingers tightly around the slender glass, to remember how to not lose hope in the middle of so much unending evil. Evil has a way of poking you like a three-year-old brother longing for attention. Poking to get a reaction, to compound all the times you've experienced it in the past, until you give up. But God knows the struggles of a riled-up mind and reminds us to keep our eyes trained on him. "Take heart," he says. "I have overcome the world."

I couldn't have known this last table, Linn's table, would break me. There was something different about this bar. All the women seemed to be crowded together instead of spread out and talking to the different men. I overlooked this and sat myself in front of them. We started talking, and the time came for me to ask if I could take one of them to dinner. I asked Sue, the woman closest to me, and with bright eyes she went to the other women and told them what I was offering. Slowly the women parted and made a clear path to a small Thai girl sitting on a stool. Hidden. It looked like tears had been streaming down her face for days. Her cheeks were chapped, and her eyes dropped. This was Linn.

The women had been hiding her because she was so young and tonight was her first night. But they knew as the night moved on they would all eventually be bought, and she would be left by herself. Their desire to hide her united with my desire to take her away. I would buy her. I would rescue her. I pulled my money out, and almost immediately the pimp emerged. A conversation ensued between the pimp and my translator. I could not buy Linn. She was going to make her pimp a lot of money that night because she was young and she was a virgin. I pulled out more money. I pulled out all my cash. I was frantic. Removing Linn became my only focus. I was so crazy with desire to show this pimp the money I could offer that I knocked over my Diet Coke. It seeped into the table, mingling with the alcohol, the evil, and the lies. My physical anchor was now a cracked cheap glass, and I had lost all peace.

The pimp stood his ground. Moments later my team was being rounded up. It was time to take the women who would come with us out to eat. I refused to leave. I didn't care if the team left without me. I was on the verge of hysteria. You don't look into a young girl's eyes and see the mark of terror and not want to tear through everything between you and her. The leader of my team eventually grabbed my arm and pulled me away. She was the head of this ministry, and she was used to seeing this. She placed me in our ride, and I burst into inconsolable tears. I could see Linn as we drove away, hope fading from her eyes.

In the car, I ran through all I had offered and wondered if I could have offered more. I was gutted by how intricate and involved of a process it was to rescue a life in bondage and realized how foolish I was to think I could come in as a savior with answers and freedom to dole out. I had not only witnessed Linn's brokenness that night, but I had also come into uncomfortable contact with my own.

It's a wild and sobering thing to behold a table prepared in the wilderness. We sit at these tables because these are the tables Jesus sat at. The tables holding wounded people with raw, breaking hearts. God seats us at these tables to be used by him as a healing balm, but he also seats us there to bring us into contact with our own brokenness. When I sat at those bar tops with those marred women, I saw that too often I chose rage as my immediate response and was quick to throw away peace in an effort to end not just the pain of others but also the pain and discomfort it caused me to see them there. But what I learned when I was forced to stay in the tension of those broken tables was that rescuing a life is not a quick solution or a well-thought-out answer. It can't be accomplished in one evening's passionate fury against the world's unjust systems. It's a long-term commitment we must choose to make if our desire is to truly partner with God in his ministry to the broken.

The mystery is that, even while staring into the face of unspeakable evil that can't be toppled in one day, we can bear peace and release peace to these tables when we remember that rescuing a life necessitates the giving of a life, something that takes investment and time. Jesus modeled this for us, and the believers of his day gawked, "You mean you aren't just going to come to the earth and slay the bad people and put yourself in charge in the high castle and allow us to enjoy the privileges that come with proclaiming you Lord?" Rather than bowing to the expectations of swift takeover and worldly kingdom building, Jesus showed, with his words and actions, that his redemption of us all would be much more costly. It would take all of him, even his very life.

When I boarded the plane to fly back to America, I sat in my seat for fourteen hours and thought about all the women I had met. I thought about Linn. I thought about her so unwaveringly that I burst into tears, and the flight attendant came over to console me. Embarrassed, I tried to steady myself and desperately reached for the peace that transcends all understanding. Then I heard the still, small whisper, *Brianne, there is no way you love Linn more than I do. No way. What you are feeling is just a drop of what I feel for her. And while you have left her, I have not.* And this is the transcending truth that allows us to sit at broken tables: God's love is fierce. And he never leaves his people.

What might the cost be if we don't continue to sit at tables shattered with the harshness of the world? What might the cost have been if Jesus hadn't? Jesus stayed steady and calculated the cost when he shared a meal with broken and forgotten people, despite the unwavering ridicule he received. His tablemates were cheaters and liars and prostitutes and broken hearts. His response to such contempt was clear and short: "Who needs a doctor: the healthy or the sick? I'm here inviting outsiders, not insiders—an invitation to a changed life, changed inside and out" (Luke 5:32 THE MESSAGE).

Because I have sat at tables with such wounded and hurting people, I know how easy it is to disengage, to not show up, or to grow despondent at the ways we can't always fix things or find a happy ending. Too often I notice how I can become hardened by the seemingly insurmountable evil in this world. But here's the thing: we know who ultimately wins this battle. We know our Rescuer's name. He is not calling us to rescue anyone; he is calling us to pull out a chair and sit amongst the broken. He is the Rescuer. We are simply an extension of his great love and peace. And he calls us to continue stepping into brokenness and gives us the strength to face the unimaginable under the banner of his love. So we must show up.

It can be difficult to continue coming to the table in the midst of the heartbreaking brokenness of others, but it can be just as difficult when the broken person at the table is yourself. I must have gone a full year broken, showing up at tables and laughing on the outside while crashing on the inside, after I returned from Thailand. I was an unlovely kind of desperate that year. I wasn't sure who I was or what I wanted. I wanted to go back to Thailand, and I wanted to stay in the comfort of America. I wanted to help hundreds, maybe thousands, of women out of prostitution. I also just wanted to go to sleep.

The problem when you're hurting is that you don't understand how visible you are. You think people can see your words and not your wounds. I thought I had become the best actress Colorado Springs had ever seen, but I would soon learn otherwise.

For some reason, that summer, I met a lot of guys. Some of them liked me, and I liked some of them. God, being the protector he is, closed the door on each one. But one guy in particular kept me distracted from my broken heart and all my confusion. Every time the door started to close on any kind of relationship we might have, I'd slide a doorstop through the crack.

I was working a full-time job at the time, but on the weekends I would drive hours to see this guy. I'd turn my music up a decibel louder than the sound of my breaking heart and roll my windows down as I drove. I loved that drive. My thoughts could never catch up to me.

After several months of escaping the town I lived in and basically becoming the adopted friend of this community that was two hours away, the curtain dropped. My performance came to a screeching halt. Every Sunday before church, this community of friends would have breakfast together. A whole house of girls and boys, everyone cooking and eating together. I felt at home. Until one girl walked up to me at breakfast on what was probably the seventh weekend in a row that I'd been there, and she cocked her head to the side and asked, "Do you live here or something? You are here every weekend. Don't you have friends where you live?"

It was exactly what I had been hoping no one would ever catch on to, that this was not my place. These were not my people. I smiled and blushed hard.

"Oh, well, I live in Colorado Springs, and all my friends have moved, and I just love the drive up here."

I should have added, "Also, I don't know where I belong. I am hurting and confused and very lost. I've seen things. Really awful things. And I was helpless in the midst of it. I was too quiet and then too angry. So, yes, I know this is not my home, but until I find it, can I please just keep running away to this place?"

She smoothed out her skirt after my timid response, seeming to take note of how exposed I felt. It was as if she were motioning with her inspection of me, *Please exit stage right.* It was then that I knew, I was only fooling myself. I felt fully and wholly uninvited. But that's the thing about making the wrong place your home. The residents start to catch on.

After church that day the guy and I went and sat in a park. I was feeling pretty heavy and pretty naked, knowing my imposter self had been exposed by at least one person. But we talked for hours about God and the hurting world and our hurting selves. He looked up at me as we folded the blanket and got ready to go. He said, "Hey, I could see myself married to you one day, and I think I'd be pretty happy." And you know what? I thought that was the best thing I'd ever heard in my whole life. That is how broken I was. The whole, "I'd be pretty happy" bit made me swoon like I had just been crowned his queen. I didn't know that one year later I'd meet someone who would get down on one knee and say, "I won't be happy until you are my wife." The contrast is so stark now in hindsight, but I couldn't see it at the time.

Convinced that this guy liked me because, you know, the whole marrying bit, I decided to keep making my trips up to his town. "What in the world was I thinking?" you might ask. Well, here's another thing I learned about hurting during that time: while most of us won't call it what it is, we are at least aware enough of the bleeding that we will decide to find some kind of bandage. I thought I'd found a tourniquet, or at least an answer to the pain. He was the drug that numbed the pain. I just needed another hit.

Exactly one week after our time on the grass, I was at his table again. We were talking, and I was forgetting everything that hurt. He walked over to the kitchen to get some drinks, and he said, "Hey, do you know Erica?" The tone in his voice alarmed me; he was being so careful with his words, like he was trying to disarm a bomb without it going off.

"Um, yeah. Yeah, I know her."

"Well, we talked this past week, and I think we're going to start dating. We think there might be something there."

Now, I'm a classy girl. So I did what classy girls do. I smiled real big and told him I was happy for him. He looked a little shocked at my reaction, which made me realize I really, really wasn't fooling anyone. I left the next morning. I was supposed to go to breakfast with the community, but there was no way I was going to eat and mingle and smile. Instead, I got up early and went to a coffee shop. I got my coffee, and I got him a coffee, the way he takes it. Then I left it at his place, a last supper of sorts. One I wouldn't stay to share with him.

I drove back to Colorado Springs and went directly to my parents' house. I marched up to my old room and buried my head in my pillow. I had never heard myself cry like I did that day. I was choking on sobs and broken pieces of my heart. My sister came into my room and grabbed my hand. "Come with me."

It was all I could do to get my legs up under me, but I followed her like she was going to take me to the well of healing. And in many ways she did. She put me in the passenger side of her car. She rolled down her windows. She cranked up the music. I threw my head into my lap and sobbed so loudly I thought I'd burst my eardrums. I was quite literally hysterical. After two hours of her allowing me to cleanse myself by emptying myself, she parked the car.

We were in the mountains. My harsh yelps of sorrow were stopped against the stark quietness of the night. The stars sparkled in a way I envied. I wanted to sparkle like that again. My sister popped open some soda cans, and we sat on the hood of the car. The crisp soda soothed my throat, and the effervescence popped on my taste buds, reminding me I could taste something else besides salt. She reached for my hand and whispered, "You are going to be okay." I looked at her, all red and wet in the face. I wanted to ask her, "How? How?!" But instead, I just trusted her.

We ended our night, and I curled up in my childhood bed. I woke up swollen and broken the next morning, but at least I knew it this time. At least I was okay with how broken I was. I stopped leaving every weekend. I started meeting people in my own town. I started inviting myself to every meal and every gathering, even though I was so shattered. I needed people. I needed community.

I have sat at many tables that I wanted to flee. It is no small thing to show up to a table when you don't even want to appear in your own life. But there is healing at the table. And I started to feel like I was home. Like every table in that town was a table I could invite myself to.

Somewhere along the way I found myself sharing bits of my story. At one table I told the story of Linn for the first time, and a new friend, one I had just met, looked at me and asked with such pure sincerity, "Are you okay?" No one up to that point had asked me if I was okay since I'd come back from Thailand. In that moment, at that table, with that question, one small piece of my heart was picked up and mounted back into place. So I kept going to the tables. And I started to notice that all those tables of brokenness were also glistening with shards of grace.

> **TIP:** A genuine way to learn how to sit at tables with broken people is to ask some trusted friends (or yourself) what they most needed when they were broken. Was it just a listening ear? Prayer? A meal dropped off?

## PRAYER FOR THE TABLE

*Jesus, you came not for the healthy but for the sick. You ate at the tables of tax collectors and sinners. May we be so willing to have the hurting at our table. May we not be made uncomfortable or distant by their hurt, but may we move ever closer to them by your power. If we are the hurting ones, give us the grace and patience to keep showing up at the table. May we all find you and usher you to our tables of brokenness.*

## QUESTIONS FOR THE TABLE

1. Have you eaten at a broken table? What was that like for you? Describe how you felt, what you thought, and where you saw Jesus in the brokenness. If you are in a season of eating at broken tables, take heart. Jesus ate at many broken tables. He knows exactly what you are facing, he sees you, and he is your anchor.
2. Do you have a story about a time when you received healing at a table? Why was there healing? Was it a kind question? Or a listening ear? Or a patient host?
3. How can you demonstrate the hope and love of Jesus at tables with the broken?

## RECIPE FOR THE TABLE

### CHICKEN CURRY WITH CAULIFLOWER RICE

Serves 4.

*Sometimes sitting at broken tables requires serving comfort food. Just as my Diet Coke became a sort of tangible anchor as I entered into long and complicated conversations in Thailand, comfort food can help anchor us. Takeout has always been my favorite comfort food—so much so that I learned how to make my own curry.*

## Ingredients:

## Curry:
1/4 cup (1/2 stick) unsalted butter
2 medium onions, finely chopped
2 large garlic cloves (or 3 small cloves), finely chopped
1 tablespoon peeled and finely minced fresh ginger
3 tablespoons curry powder
2 teaspoons salt
1 teaspoon ground cumin
1/2 teaspoon cayenne pepper (optional)
2 (8-ounce) boneless, skinless chicken breasts, cut into 1-inch
    cubes
1 (14.5-ounce) can diced tomatoes
3/4 cup full-fat canned coconut cream
3/4 cup cashews, finely ground

## Cauliflower Rice:
1 head cauliflower
1/4 cup chicken stock
1 teaspoon garlic powder
1 1/2 teaspoons salt
1 cup golden raisins
1/4 cup roughly chopped cashews

## Instructions:
To prepare the curry, heat the butter in a large skillet over medium-low heat until it is melted and slightly bubbling. Add the onions, garlic, and ginger. Cook and stir until softened, about 5 minutes.

Add the curry powder, salt, cumin, and cayenne (omit the cayenne if you do not like spicy curry), and cook, stirring to coat the onion mixture with the spices, for 1 minute.

Add the chicken, and cook, stirring to coat, for 3 minutes.

Add the tomatoes, including the juice, and bring the mixture to a simmer. Cover and allow to simmer for 20 minutes, stirring occasionally.

Uncover and add the coconut cream. Stir, cover, and simmer for 20 minutes, stirring occasionally.

Add the finely ground cashews. Stir and cook for 5 minutes.

To prepare the cauliflower rice, wash and dry the cauliflower. Remove the greens, and cut the head into 4 sections.

To grate the cauliflower, use a box grater or a food processor with the grater attachment.

Add the grated cauliflower to a medium pot, along with the chicken stock, garlic powder, and salt. Turn the heat to medium, cover, and allow to steam for 7 minutes. Uncover and stir to fluff. Stir in the raisins and chopped cashews.

Serve the curry over the cauliflower rice.

NOTE: You can also use basmati rice in place of the cauliflower rice. Follow the instructions on the package, and add the raisins and cashews at the end. Serve the curry over the rice.

To see pictures of this recipe, visit http://oursavorylife.com/chicken-curry-recipe-paleo-rice/.

## TRICK

Bringing your pan to the right temperature before adding meat helps the meat not stick to the pan. A great trick to know if your pan is heated properly is to slightly tip it and see if the oil in the pan creates long legs. If so, it's time to add your meat. You will know it is time to flip your meat when it easily pulls away from the pan (without sticking) as you flip it.

# six

# HOSPITALITY AT THE TABLE

*The ideal flower of hospitality is almost unknown*
*to the rich; it can hardly be grown save in the*
*gardens of the poor; it is one of their beatitudes.*

—GEORGE MACDONALD

Almost everything I've learned about undefiled hospitality, I learned from the poor. It is one thing to give out of our abundance; it is another thing to give from our lack. Entertaining friends and people with whom I am comfortable, especially when I have stuff to give, is a lot like what Jesus said about loving people, "For if you love those who love you, what reward do you have? Do not even the tax collectors do the same? And if you greet only your brothers, what more are you doing than others? Do not even the Gentiles do the same?" (Matthew 5:46–47). A refining happens when we fling open our doors to those we do not understand or know or who do not live in our financial bracket. It's not just a nice idea to invite the poor and the overlooked; it was Jesus' consistent desire for our tables.

> Then he [Jesus] turned to the host. "The next time you put on a dinner, don't just invite your friends and family and rich neighbors, the kind of people who will return the favor. Invite some people who never get invited out, the misfits from the wrong side of the tracks. You'll be—and experience—a blessing. They won't be able to return the favor, but the favor will be returned—oh, how it will be returned!—at the resurrection of God's people." (Luke 14:12–14 THE MESSAGE)

*Hospitality* translated from the Greek means "love of strangers." God's economy scarcely runs without strong enticement for us to show great generosity to the stranger, the outsider, and the marginalized. It's a thread that runs from the Old Testament straight through to the New Testament.

> You shall treat the stranger who sojourns with you as the native among you, and you shall love him as yourself, for you were strangers in the land of Egypt: I am the LORD your God. (Leviticus 19:34)

> For I was hungry and you gave me food, I was thirsty and you gave me drink, I was a stranger and you welcomed me, I was naked and you clothed me, I was sick and you visited me, I was in prison and you came to me. (Matthew 25:35–36)

> [God] executes justice for the fatherless and the widow, and *loves the sojourner, giving him food and clothing.* Love the sojourner,

therefore, for you were sojourners in the land of Egypt. (Deuteronomy 10:18–19, emphasis mine)

Do not neglect to show hospitality to strangers, for thereby some have entertained angels unawares. (Hebrews 13:2)

Loving a stranger is the one great act that proclaims we are all here together, in this world together, banged up and busted. In doing so, we acknowledge our oneness. We recognize that God chose to create every single person on this earth, his hand forming and placing each one of us in this hard and striking land, saying, *walk together.* We look at someone whose background we might not know, whose trials we've not yet heard of, whose sins we have not yet seen, and we say, "Come a little closer. You look familiar. You look like God." We all, each of us, bear the image of God. And we all can be used as an outpouring of his generosity. Sitting at the feet of the poor and accepting blessing from out of their deficiency has humbled me. It has shown me that the hospitality God honors is not necessarily the one where we give from the overflow of our stuff but the one where we give of ourselves. This can get messy, which is the case whenever we open our hearts to one another, but, then again, if true hospitality isn't at least a little bit messy, then maybe we're doing it wrong?

On Wednesday, August 3, 2016, I had a meal with three-year-old Esther in Bolivia.

Esther lives in extreme poverty in the south of Cochabamba with her grandmother and grandfather, her three sisters, and her mother, Inez. I was leading a team to Bolivia that summer as part of Compassion International's blogger program, and the plan that day was to visit Esther and her family. When we arrived at her home, we all huddled into one room. Esther sat there so quiet that she instantly became the loudest presence in the room. While her sister, Genesis, roamed around and honored us with her smile and giggles (the kind of giggle you want to hear for the rest of your life), Esther sat there timid, almost willing herself to be smaller. Her grandmother, Eulogio, shared their story with us, a story of abuse and robbery and the severe lack of daily food. We all took heavy breaths and let Eulogio rest in stuttering sobs. This was another table of brokenness, or so I thought.

Eventually Eulogio stood up and gathered the family to sing to us. They grabbed their hymn book and sang loudly. Because that's what you do when the darkness starts to suffocate. You sing. When you are giving from a place of openness and hospitality, you offer not just your brokenness but your hope as well. This is something I've seen whenever I've spent time with the poor. I have seen them love me, a stranger at first, by sitting me at their table and sharing their brokenness. I've seen them build a bridge to me and my humanness by revealing their maze of a journey on this earth. And I've seen them break open their hope and invite me to see God's goodness in the middle of it all. So often the poor are masters at hospitality because they don't have the luxury (or is it the burden?) of offering anything beyond themselves. They only have their one shattered heart to give. They can't hide behind overstuffed couches, nice-smelling candles, or perfectly roasted chicken.

Back in Bolivia, the chicken empanadas arrived, and everyone shuffled around the room a bit, finding new seats as the napkins and cups were handed out. The spot next to Esther became open, and before I really knew what I was going to say or do, I was in that empty seat right next to her. She looked away from me immediately. She crunched smaller into herself, and I thought about moving. Was I scaring her? Was I making her uncomfortable? But before I could decide on my next move, the wet wipes arrived for us to wash our hands.

Esther took her napkin and barely brushed the top of one hand before discarding it to her side. My inner mama bear took over, and suddenly there I was, picking up her wet wipe and gently lifting her hand to do a more thorough cleaning. Very slowly and very carefully I took each hand and scrubbed. As I washed them she inched closer to me. I weaved in between her fingers and polished her nails. She looked closely as each shiny nail was revealed after the wipe had brushed it clean.

It occurred to me in that moment that because this family had welcomed us so fully into their lives and had done the hard work of loving me even though I was a stranger, it was not unnatural for me to lean into Esther like she was my own and wash away her dirt. Sometimes to feel safe with someone we need them to see our dirt and be gentle with us. We need them to grab a napkin and carefully help us wipe it away. We need someone to show us that the dirt isn't permanent. It's not who we are; it's just something we picked up while living our story. Most of the time it really helps when a stranger comes along and shows us how removable the dirt can be. It's about being kind and helpful. It's about freeing us all up to walk a little closer to one another because of the love Jesus has for us. This is the beginning of loving a stranger. When we boast in God and not ourselves, the dirt of others does not repel us; it compels us.

After we cleaned our hands, the Coke came and was poured into glasses like a shining communion. The family sang one more song to thank God for the meal. Their praise echoed through the mudroom we sat in, and I marveled at the offering this family had brought to the Lord. Their hospitality was not limited by our presence, though we had only just met. Instead, it seemed to be illuminated by it. We received the chicken empanadas, and all fell silent as we broke open the flaky crust with thankful mouths.

Do you know how long it takes to drink a soda and eat an empanada that is smaller than a McDonald's cheeseburger? It took Esther nearly forty minutes. She cradled her soda and took the most grateful sips. Every swallow ended with a smile and that irresistible "aah" sound. She finally moved on to the empanada and ate it slowly, like she needed it to last the whole day. I watched as the team and family members finished their food and began to shuffle around, moving outside and then eventually heading back inside. But not Esther. She sat there happy, enthralled with her empanada. And I just couldn't get up and leave while she was thoroughly relishing her meal. I was so honored to share that meal with her. It was amazing how this family, living in the raw despair of poverty, had made me feel fully welcomed and loved. How they gave from their poverty—not in spite of it. How they took us from strangers to neighbors by pulling up what seemed like an X-ray of their slashed-through hearts and pointing out all the places they were broken but also mended by hope. When you don't have fancy meals, long wooden tables, or frilly doilies, you offer all you *can* give, which, in the end, is the best thing to give: your heart.

The table marked with hospitality is seasonless. It should appear in all times. In seasons of bounty and seasons of need. Seasons of joy and seasons of brokenness. When we lay our table with hospitality, we are not looking to ourselves for provision. God can use us to give in times of poverty and in times of bounty. But regardless of the season, our table of hospitality proclaims, "Come in. I do not know your name, but I know your maker. And so, I offer you my heart." We must align our presence and our purpose for the table and for our homes with our allegiance to Christ. Jesus called the stranger to the table. And he did not just invite the stranger and feed him; he had great love for him. So must we.

Though we may have the best intentions to welcome the stranger, some days this may seem harder than others. There was one day recently when heaviness seemed to latch onto my soul. All around me was gray and a humming of uselessness. These days are rare for my usually upbeat, radically optimistic self, but, for some reason, on this day all my usual tricks were not working. So I decided to be very, very gentle with myself.

I sat at my table and proceeded to lavish hospitality on myself. I wrote and read for hours. I cooked an incredibly savory, bountiful breakfast for myself. I polished off two cups of coffee. But, after all that, I looked around at the world, and it all still seemed shapeless. So I proceeded to walk to the edge of the ocean. I needed to stand on the hem of something bigger than me. Right there on the edge, I seemed to find my place in the world. Small but not insignificant. Healing was coming. I then proceeded to walk to the local coffee shop and purchase an iced coffee. I had now entered the realm of showing extreme kindness to myself. But despite my excellent choices for self-care, and though my perspective was shifting, I still seemed to flap like a fish out of water. I thought, *I need radical hospitality shown to me.*

And then I heard the Holy Spirit, hushed and still: *You and everyone else. Get up!*

So, right there, I made a list of a few random acts of kindness that I could practice that day. I wanted to show extreme, unencumbered love to strangers. I was taking the words of Anne Lamott seriously: "We get to start our new twenty-four hours every time we remember."[1] So, after spiraling and blinking too many times (like I was trying to put the world back into focus), I remembered

Jesus. I remembered that anything I want to hungrily pull from heaven down to earth starts with his command, to love him and to love others.

I heeded the Holy Spirit's instruction to get up and marched to the counter to purchase some gift cards. The guy at the cash register instructed, "You should buy these tomorrow. We will have great designs for our gift cards tomorrow!"

I whispered carefully, "Oh, no. We need these gift cards today." *The world needs love today.* Then I started my walk home. It would take twenty minutes. I had twenty minutes to hand out my gift cards. And then I met Michael.

He looked homeless, a suitcase next to him, dirty clothes hanging loosely. I approached him slowly and watched as his wrinkled, sun-dried hand acted like a mop on his forehead, brushing the sweat from his brow.

"Excuse me, sir?" I spoke gently and slowly, not wanting to startle or offend this man.

"Oh . . . oh, hello there," he responded slowly. I watched him blink in rapid succession like he, too, was trying to put this world into some kind of focus. Trying to make sense of it. He was a stranger for sure. A sojourner on this earth who never did pull it together enough to get on with the way things work here.

"Hi, how are you today?" I smiled big and tried to convey my innocence.

"Oh, well, I . . . I guess. Well, I am okay. I guess . . ." He trailed off like he had been trying to find the answer to that question his whole life.

"Well, I was just walking by and I have this gift card to the coffee shop right down there, and I was hoping you might want it?" I stretched out my hand, and as he latched onto the card there seemed to be a bridge between us. Our paths crossing in this big wide world.

He then erupted with stories from his past, opening his heart like he'd been practicing this kind of emotional hospitality his whole life. After a few moments we both stood, quieted. We exchanged names, and I went on my way. As I routed my steps back to my home, I felt tears come down my face, and the blurriness of the world sharpened and filled with color.

Michael and I had both participated in radical kindness. He had opened the proverbial door to his little patch of dirt, though I was a stranger. He received me with gentleness and accepted my small offering with great joy. He shared his stories, which were hard-won and scarcely conquered. He showed me a new kind of hospitality, the kind God created.

As I reflected on this experience, I decided I was going to return and take meals to Michael. Over the next few days, I would show up to his little patch of dirt and serve him a meal. Outwardly, it might have seemed as if I was ministering to him, but this is how God's kingdom works: I'm pretty certain I needed Michael's hospitality more than he needed mine. Michael might have wanted the meal I brought him, but I needed his stories. I needed to be welcomed and loved by Michael because it pulled me out of the pettiness of my day and my worries. He allowed me to be what I so desire to be with my life, the hands and feet of Jesus. And he was Jesus right back to me.

> **TIP:** *Hospitality* literally means "love of strangers." Think of one way this week you can show love to a stranger. This might mean buying groceries or coffee for the person behind you in line. Or maybe giving a compliment to a random person who crosses your path.

Sharing a meal with a stranger is a radical lesson in, "We are all here together. For better or for worse. Why not for better? Why not walk together? Let's walk each other out of this foreign land and straight to the door that leads us home." For me it was this wild opportunity to unlearn the hospitality of the world.

The world says, "Hospitality can only be shown by those who have the nice home, the bigger table, the bone china." God's hospitality says, "It's best if you give from your poverty, not from your abundance."

The world says, "Worry about yourself first; no one is looking out for you but you." God's hospitality says, "If you lose your life for me and for others, you will save it."

The world's hospitality says, "What delicious food will we serve?" God's hospitality says, "I have my one slashed-through heart that is broken that I may give of it, and it is the best thing I will be able to give."

True godly hospitality must become a message we live. A message that leaks out of us. If you have not encountered the economy of God's hospitality, get out of your house and start with receiving from the poor. Yes, receive from the poor. Maybe you give some cash to a homeless man on the street. Maybe you bring a bottle of water and a sandwich to a woman on the corner. You will think you are giving, but be vigilant because you are about to receive in a way you may not have experienced. Believe me when I say that starting here will completely transform how you show hospitality at your table. It will humble you; it will make you more vulnerable. You will listen harder. You will speak softer.

One evening I was bringing a meal to Michael, and I saw a man emerging from the place where Michael keeps his stuff. I was so overjoyed to witness another human giving to Michael, and before I could gather my thoughts, I ran after the man. "Excuse me. Do you know Michael?"

The guy turned to me and, a little shocked, explained, "I have never met him. He is always asleep when I come by, but I give him a meal every evening."

I let out what must have been such breathy wisps of hope and explained, "I give Michael a meal every morning."

The gentleman smiled big and said, "I'm bringing him a blanket tomorrow."

I responded, "I am bringing him a cane in the morning."

We stood quietly, then shook hands and turned back onto our respective paths. When God's people are acting out of a heart of hospitality, when they are practicing it at their tables and receiving it from the tables of the poor, there is unity and love that can break the chains of sin and injustice.

We don't have to complicate the practice of hospitality at our tables. It can be whittled down to two simple words: *love strangers*. We can start on the outside, learning by receiving and being open to a change in perspective. A meal with the poor on their turf. Maybe accepting an invitation from someone you don't know well or who is vastly different from you. Hospitality is the great equalizer. God uses it to humble us and return us to meekness. When we feel that our focus has slightly shifted from the great work God has for us here, we can realign and refocus by loving a stranger into a neighbor and inviting them to our tables.

The beautiful thing about engaging in hospitality is we get to practice it out of our own unique gifting. God made us all intricately wonderful and different. My hospitality will look different from your hospitality. But I didn't learn to fully lean into this until Jeremy and I moved and we became new neighbors.

Jeremy and I had been living in our new home in Hermosa Beach for about two months, but we still had not met our next-door neighbors. A huge bush covered the side of their house, so we rarely ever saw them enter or leave their home. In fact, it was starting to seem like they were never home. The only time we knew they were afoot was early in the morning when they would take their dog for a walk. It was starting to feel like an uncomfortable situation. We hadn't yet formally met them, but every morning when they walked their dog they were assaulted by our dog's loud barks.

One evening Jeremy and I were sitting on our patio eating our meal. Our patio is on the front of our home, and we love eating there because it exponentially increases our opportunities to invite others over. Everyone can see us. Everyone can smell our food! Anyway, we were there eating, and we heard the neighbor's door close. Predictably, Stout (our dog) lost his ever-loving mind. Jeremy and I quickly grabbed Stout and took him inside to calm him down and train him not to bark at the other dog (to this day, we are still trying to train him in this). We returned to our table to see that our neighbors had disappeared into the park. Jeremy and I decided it was time. Drastic measures needed to be taken. Twenty minutes later, as they rounded the corner of the park on their way back, I called out to them.

"Excuse me! Hello, neighbors!"

Nothing. Apparently they did not hear me. So I called out again.

"Hellooooooo! Neighbors!"

They both looked up, and I suddenly realized I didn't know what to say from there. Fortunately, words still tumbled from my mouth: "We really do like you! Sorry our dog barks every time you leave the house. We'd love to have a meal with you!"

Jeremy looked at me with curiosity. If you know me you know that I basically like all people, so this statement was not necessarily unwarranted, but I'm sure it sounded strange to these people who had never met us. They ended up coming to our patio, and we talked for a bit. They brought over their dog and big smiles.

"We want to hang out with you too! We've been out of town so much these past few months, but we're back for the rest of the summer. Let's get together!"

We said a hearty good evening to one another, and they continued their walk. It felt great to be so authentically myself in my extension of hospitality. Some people knock on doors with muffins. Some people send out paper invitations. Not me. I shout out to you about how much I like you.

A few nights later we decided to officially invite our neighbors over, but I raided the pantry and found we had very little to offer. That day was supposed to have been a grocery shopping day, but I'd gotten caught up in life. We thought about having them over the next night when we would have a proper meal, but then I thought about what God has so consistently taught me as I have received hospitality from the poor: We do not have to give from our abundance. We can give what we have and give of ourselves.

So Jeremy and I raided our cheese drawer. Do not even get me started on our cheese drawer. We always have at least four different cheeses on hand. Cheese is a food group. (Please, no one ever let me be in charge of the official food pyramid. So far I have placed salsa and cheese as prominent categories.) I dusted off a big cutting board, and we loaded it up with sharp Cheddar, tangy goat, crumbly Gorgonzola, and soft, pillowy Brie. Then we added almonds, and I grabbed an apple and sliced it up. We had some blackberry jam that I dolloped onto the goat cheese, and then we scattered water crackers throughout the board.

Satisfied with our creation, Jeremy went over and knocked on our neighbors' door, but no one was there. So he promptly returned and invaded my office for a sticky note. He wrote,

"Cheese tray——>!" with the arrow pointing to our patio and left the note on their door. This was so great, because this type of hospitality matched Jeremy's personality just like my effusive invitation matched mine. Jeremy loves notes, and he is also rather to the point in his communication style. We took the cheese tray out to the patio with bottles of crisp sparkling water, and about thirty minutes later they arrived! We ate cheese and talked for three hours. Since then we have become great friends.

The table dressed in hospitality looks to the Giver of all things for provision, not to our stuff. The table marked with hospitality says, "You will come as a stranger and leave as a neighbor." The table that we root in loving strangers reminds us that we are all here, marked up with the image of God, all sojourners in this foreign land just trying to get home. And maybe it would be nice if we shared meals as we journey along.

## PRAYER FOR THE TABLE

*Jesus, thank you for letting us participate in your great work. Thank you for calling us to extend ourselves and our food and to trust you with everything else. May we do the holy and honored work of practicing hospitality, so that we might be your hands and feet to a hurting world. Amen.*

## QUESTIONS FOR THE TABLE

1. Have you ever received gracious hospitality from the poor? Describe your encounter.
2. What are some unique ways God has gifted you to show hospitality?
3. What is one way you can love a stranger this month?

# RECIPE FOR THE TABLE

## IT'S DONE ALREADY?
## CHICKEN SALSA SOUP

**Serves 5 to 6.**

*This soup is a one-pot wonder, and it takes minutes from start to finish. It's perfect for last-minute guests and a great way to keep you out of the kitchen and, instead, at the table.*

## Ingredients:
1 tablespoon olive oil
1/2 medium white onion, diced
2 garlic cloves, diced
6 cups chicken stock or chicken broth
Juice of 2 limes
2 cups shredded rotisserie or precooked chicken
1 (15-ounce) can white cannellini beans, drained (optional)
1 cup frozen corn (optional)
1 (16-ounce) jar tomatillo salsa
Toppings for serving, such as hot sauce, sour cream, shredded
    Cheddar cheese, fresh cilantro, sliced avocado, and lime wedges

## Instructions:
Heat a large pot or Dutch oven over medium-high heat. Add the olive oil, and when the oil is hot, add the diced onion and garlic. Cook, stirring, for about 3 minutes, until the onion is softened.

Add the chicken broth, lime juice, shredded chicken, beans, corn, and salsa.

Allow the soup to simmer for 10 to 15 minutes, stirring occasionally. To serve, let your guests ladle out some soup, and have toppings set out for them to add to the soup.

## TRICK ———————————————————————————

My favorite last-minute dinnertime hack is to buy a whole, roasted chicken. Pull the meat off the chicken, and divide it in half. Place half the shredded chicken in a freezer-safe plastic bag, and store for up to one month in the freezer. Take the other half and use it to quickly make a flavorful soup or a quick fajita stir-fry.

*seven*

# PEACE AT THE TABLE

*Peace is a daily, a weekly, a monthly process,
gradually changing opinions, slowly eroding old
barriers, quietly building new structures.*

—JOHN F. KENNEDY

If you were to ask me about my earliest memory of food around the table, I'd tell you about that time I was seven. I'd tell you about Lucky Charms.

My sister and I were angry, our little hearts bubbling with hurt. I'm not sure what we were mad about, but the only answer seemed to be to run away. We vented loudly about our plan as we packed our tiny backpacks. We weren't trying to sneak out; we were trying to send a message. And we were going to send that message by walking out the front door in broad daylight.

We flung open the front door, proclaiming, "Goodbye!" But before our tiny feet went from home to the outside world, my mom emerged from the kitchen. Calm and gentle as ever, holding two bowls of our favorite cereal. We predicted she was about to plead for us to stay, but she simply invited us to eat.

"Before you go on your long journey, perhaps you want to have some breakfast first? Surely you will need some nourishment. And then you can be on your way."

My sister and I looked at each other, both starting to feel the growl of our tummies. Yes, food first. We dropped our bags and sat at the table, spooning cereal into our mouths. What was breakfast for us was a gracious offer of nourishment and a nudge toward peace from my mom. Whatever we were upset about seemed to fall into the pit of our stomachs with that meal. Sweet conversation arose, perhaps sweeter than the milk after all that cereal was gone. We lingered. After we got up from the table, we decided that perhaps today was not a good day to run away. It might rain. Or, maybe by the time we got on with it, lunchtime would be nearing. And how could we go on a long journey without lunch? So we unpacked our bags and settled in. To my recollection, we never tried to run away again.

That was the first meal I received as a peace offering, a meal that didn't primarily serve as physical nourishment, but instead was used as a pathway to peace. This is the power of a meal, even something as simple as a bowl of cereal, and my mom knew it. Jesus knew it too. I think he knew food could be used to proclaim peace every time he stepped into a tax collector's home. He knew food could be used to offer peace every time he reclined at a table with those who were known as notorious sinners. He joined them in the necessary and vulnerable act of eating a meal, and through that he brought peace.

Jesus can also show up and bring peace through graham crackers and milk at midnight. Believe me, I would know.

When my sister and I were little, the ending of the day was a mysterious form of catastrophe. The end of the day meant bedtime and sleep, which only seemed to beckon another new day forward. A new unwanted school day. Another exhausted walk to the bus stop. Sleepy eyes being rubbed open on the ride to school. More homework. To participate willingly in beckoning more of this seemed not only illogical but, on one particular night, simply out of the question.

So how does a little one prolong the night? Well, they get hungry. They get thirsty. They have to go to the bathroom . . . at least three times.

Our strategy that night? Hunger. We pleaded for food well after our bedtime. I'm sure we acted as if we hadn't eaten for days. I'm sure our repetitious pleas ranged from sweet, doe-eyed requests to absolute hysteria. "We're staaaaaaarving!" we lamented, but ultimately we were sent to our rooms. We crawled under our covers, shocked that our parents would risk sending half-starved children to bed. Just as we were admitting defeat, our door opened. Our dad stepped in carrying a tray filled with graham crackers and milk. My sister and I bounded out of bed and gathered on the floor to eat this unexpected meal together. My dad sat with us, dipping the crisp cracker into the milk and swirling it for the exact right time to produce a soft-but-not-too-soggy piece of graham cracker. We laughed as we ate, and then we went to bed, a little less overwhelmed by what tomorrow would hold.

Looking back, I know my dad was certain we were not actually starving. My parents had every right to turn down our pleas and send us to bed, but I wonder if they could sense the heaviness in our hearts that night. I wonder if they saw that peace was not climbing into bed with us, so they presented space for peace with food. With those simple elements on a tray, we caught a glimpse of God's love for us as a Father through this gracious act from our own earthly father. We were reminded that night, and now constantly through the memory, that God knows exactly what we need. And sometimes, a lot of times, he emerges with a symbolic meal at hand even if it's not necessary. Even if it's just to spend a little time with his children and remind us that we can hush and settle and let his peace carry us through the night. Surely he, too, brings figurative plates of graham crackers into our lives, if just to remind us that his love goes far beyond necessity.

I can't remember ever having a first day of school when I came home to an empty table. I think, in a lot of ways, my mom knew she was sending us out into a hard, hurting world—one she could not fully protect us from—so she seemed to always want to make sure we knew that home would be a place of peace, of safety. Mom did that with food.

The first day of school was always a challenge for me. I was a little wisp of a thing growing up. Very petite and small. My mom tells how, when I was in elementary school, she would watch me climb, literally climb, the school bus steps, and then I would disappear, too small to be seen through the windows of the large bus. On one of my first days riding the bus home, my mom waited eagerly at my stop for me to disembark and, to her initial terror, did not see me get off. The bus driver motioned my mom to come forward; she peeked inside the bus and could barely see my hand held high above the seat. The bus driver said firmly, "Ma'am, I asked if this was anyone's stop, and she raised her hand. Please make sure to tell her she also needs to get off the bus." I was small, and I was timid. School was very unforgiving for the likes of me.

I guess, to kids, small meant a lot of things. A lot of hurtful things. Sometimes it meant ugly, and other times it meant stupid. Most days in those younger years I would come home crying, and my mom would cry with me as I told her some of the hurtful things that were hurled in my direction. My dad would hold my hand, and we'd all deflate a little bit under the weight of those words. The problem with hateful words is they usually slam into their target at full speed and lodge securely, like they have found a new home. I carried those hurtful words for a long time. As the school year went on, though, I found friends, and the days grew less frightful. But the school year always ended, and then it always started back up again the following year. My mom's routine of having some delicious snack ready at the end of the first day of school always made it less awful. I knew peace was in our home, at our table.

Often on those first days I'd find myself wondering throughout the day what she would have for us. A cheese plate? A plate full of veggies with my favorite dressing? A slice of her incredible three-layer chocolate cake? As I rounded the corner with my brother and sister, my mom would be on the back porch, waiting, holding a platter of something delicious, an extension of her love and hope for us. It wasn't just nourishment; it was peace in the middle of troubling circumstances. I would fill my stomach with delicious morsels of food, and my heart seemed to fill back up too.

I carry these stories of how God has used food as a proffering of peace in my life. They are like a distant memory, swaying back and forth in my heart. A bit blurry but present. And when I need to remember how God heals and provides an unshakable sense of his loving presence in difficult moments, how he blesses me with his peace, I look to those memories—those moments Jesus showed up and stood right next to my mom, helping her hold the meal and waving with her as I rounded the corner home from school.

My parents' efforts to consistently foster peace at the table made a remarkable impact on me as I grew up. This peace would be the one I ran to the first time I truly came unraveled.

At eighteen I was still trying to find my place in Christianity, still trying to understand who I really was (this was the height of my people-pleasing phase, so you can imagine what a hard time I was having trying to figure myself out while making sure everyone around me liked me). I worked at a restaurant at that time where I was the only believer, but I loved the group of servers. So I played the game. In the evenings I would hang out with my friends from Campus Crusade for Christ, but late at night I would sneak away and go hang out with my other group of friends. I always felt a little less intimidated with these friends. Less like I needed to perform. Everyone was just up for having a good time, man.

At that point in my life, I was still trying to decide what to dabble in: Alcohol? Drugs? Sex? It was all available to me, but I was still playing the spectator (for reasons I still do not understand except that God had his job cut out for him as protector and he excelled). Until this one night. I was at a friend's house for a birthday party, and everyone was having, as you can imagine, a very good time. I was not interested in drinking, but there was some punch that looked delicious. Of course I knew the punch was spiked, but I was not really interested in the actual punch. I just wanted the fruit. The fruit sitting there at the bottom of the bowl looked juicy and plump. My mouth watered a little, and I thought for sure the fruit was only slightly tainted with alcohol. I took the ladle for the punch and carefully plopped heaps of the fruit into my cup and proceeded to munch on it throughout the night. At one point, the point when I started wondering why I couldn't stand up and my sentences were coming out a little funny, my friend came up and spouted, "Are *you* drunk?" The idea was obviously preposterous. I wasn't even drinking.

"No! I just ate fruit . . . yummy fruit from the bottom of that punch bowl."

My friend quickly educated me on what happens to the fruit in spiked punch. It soaks up most of the alcohol. I was probably putting more alcohol into my system by eating the fruit than I would have by drinking the punch. As you can imagine, this was quite alarming to me. I felt my whole being start to unravel as I started to berate myself and realize that I wasn't sure how long I would be conscious. My next action was immediate. I needed to return to a sense of peace. I needed to remember who I was. I marched up to my friend's room, picked up her phone, and called my parents. They picked up. They always pick up.

"Hi, Bri! Are you okay?" they asked gently, as they had probably glanced at their clock to see it was around midnight. Just the sound of their voices settled and grounded me. Peace picked up the phone.

"Yes, I would like to come home. Can you please come pick me up?"

They arrived about ten minutes later. I expected questions on the drive home, maybe a small interrogation, but that never came. They only said one thing the whole drive home: "Thank you for calling us."

This natural instinct to go to my parents when I desperately needed a place of safety and peace was first forged at our table. Mom and Dad had done the hard work of regularly bringing us together and being available to us. They had invested the time and the heart to cultivate that environment of peace, so all these years later, when I got myself into trouble, the first thing I thought to do was to call them, a choice most of my peers would have thought was crazy.

By practicing peace at the table, we can foster a deep sense of steadiness in a world that brings great chasms into our lives and the lives of the people we love. If we can take this fruit of the Spirit and begin the holy work of bringing it consistently to our tables, I believe we can transform our relationships. Peace won't just be a guest that shows up at our tables; it will become an outpouring of our lives. We will become a place of safety, and maybe at times a place of rescue, when the world bats hard.

Peace is undeniably important to Jesus. According to the *Holman Bible Dictionary*, the word *peace* occurs in every New Testament book except 1 John.[1] The term is not to be understood as simply the opposite of war or hostility but as "a condition and sense of being safe and secure."[2] Ultimately, we can reveal the gracious and wondrous peace we have in God as we steward peace at our tables.

The apostle Peter seemed to be a man who needed the peace of God repeatedly—especially in those days following the crucifixion of his beloved Master.

After Jesus' sacrifice and the weeklong Feast of Unleavened Bread, the disciples left Jerusalem and returned to Galilee. I wonder if it all felt like one big adventure that had ended with too many questions and the unimaginable, gaping void of Jesus' presence. Peter and the disciples went back to the existence they'd had before Jesus had banged loudly into their lives. Maybe they were groping for a little familiarity after such a heart-shattering and, ultimately, humanity-shattering week. Failure can drape any vestige of peace in a dark, thick veil, leaving a heart without a compass.

I can only imagine what Peter must have felt as he stayed up late into the night, fishing, participating in an activity that belonged to his former life, before Jesus had called him. Maybe he felt like he had lost his way. After all, he knew he had forsaken his Lord. Peter, the devout and confidently committed disciple, found his last stand for Jesus soaked in denial. Repeated denial. Denial just the way Jesus had predicted it. It must have been a night of mental gymnastics, tossing and turning with regret and failure. Maybe he wished for a do-over.

That night had to have been long, but maybe Peter found comfort in the familiar sway of the boat in the water. Maybe he thought, *This is where I belong. This is what I know.* And what sorrow daylight must have brought when he found his net empty and saw failure even where he had once been an expert. But the thing about Jesus is, he overcomes. And he shows up in this gray scene. He comes with a meal.

> Jesus said, "Breakfast is ready." Not one of the disciples dared ask, "Who are you?" They knew it was the Master.
>
> Jesus then took the bread and gave it to them. He did the same with the fish. This was now the third time Jesus had shown himself alive to the disciples since being raised from the dead. (John 21:12–13 THE MESSAGE)

What an outbreak of peace and comfort Peter must have experienced when he saw his Christ on the shore, preparing a meal of bread and fish. This would not be a short encounter. It would be one of provision. Lingering. Eating. Conversation. Jesus fed Peter's weary body after a night of laboring, relying on his own efforts. And then Jesus reinstated Peter, reminding Peter to feed his sheep and creating space for Peter to proclaim three times that he loved Jesus. Three times, each one an eraser for the three denials he'd voiced at Jesus' trial.

I sometimes wonder why, during Jesus' repetitive question to Peter, "Do you love me more than these?" Peter never interjected and asked, "But, Lord, do you still love me?" Peter had to have known that even though his rejection was severe and threefold, Jesus' love was absolute and never changing.

Peter sat on that sandy beach with Jesus, shoveling pieces of flaky fish into his mouth, and he knew his Savior brought peace. Peter went looking for fish all night, and Jesus met him with more fish than he could have imagined. At that table on the beach, Jesus conveyed, "You're still mine." He broke bread with Peter and affirmed, "My broken body is for you too." Surely that day Peter put away his fishing net for good. Surely that day Jesus took Peter's deflated and scarred heart and said, "I still call you to great things." And he did this all beside the fire of a meal. A meal presented as an offer of peace to calm the turmoil in Peter's heart.

**TIP:** Cultivating peace at the table is first and foremost an overflow of the peace we experience from God. Take time this week to lean into and walk in the peace God offers you. Meditate on Romans 8:1.

If my table could look like this scene for my loved ones, it would be grand. To call my weary people to the table for a time of peaceful refreshing, complete with a meal that will nourish. To sit with them in their hurt and restlessness and what they feel might be failure at the end of the day. To remind them that Jesus calls them to great things. To take the net of their day and exchange it for his peace. That would be the greatest privilege.

Jesus knew how to host a meal. Even one on a sandy beach with a few fish and a loaf of bread. The meal didn't have to be extravagant, because Jesus' love was. Jesus' love still is. And that's all we need to walk in complete peace and assurance.

## PRAYER FOR THE TABLE

*Father, we come to you just as we are. We come home after a day at war with our flesh. We come home feeling like we may have lost a few battles, like we missed the mark of your calling. But we look to you for our peace tonight. We look to you because we know you have not forsaken us. You have not called us back to our former life apart from you, but you draw us ever nearer, reminding us that we do, in fact, love you more than this world and what it has to offer. Fill us with your peace that reminds us you won the war. Fill us with your peace as we share a meal.*

## QUESTIONS FOR THE TABLE

1. Do you have a memory of receiving a meal that brought great peace? Was that peace the result of the company or the food itself, or both?
2. What do you most want people to leave your table feeling? Is it peace? Did you find peace at your table growing up? How can we usher the peace of God to our table? The peace that pardons us, that reminds us we are covered by his sacrifice, that is Jesus' voice to us, saying,

> Are you tired? Worn out? Burned out on religion? Come to me. Get away with me and you'll recover your life. I'll show you how to take a real rest. Walk with me and work with me—watch how I do it. Learn the unforced rhythms of grace. I won't lay anything heavy or ill-fitting on you. Keep company with me and you'll learn to live freely and lightly. (Matthew 11:28–30 THE MESSAGE)

## RECIPE FOR THE TABLE

## CILANTRO LIME FISH TACOS

Serves 4 to 5.

*In honor of the meal Jesus ate and prepared several times, let's make fish! Mahi mahi is a mild-tasting fish with a firm texture that makes it great for grilling. These tacos are filled with flavor thanks to the marinade. People who don't like fish have told me they love this meal.*

## Ingredients:

2 garlic cloves, peeled
1 cup cilantro leaves, loosely packed
Juice of 2 limes
2 teaspoons ground cumin
1 1/2 teaspoons kosher salt
1 teaspoon freshly ground black pepper
1 pound mahi mahi
Oil for the grill
Corn tortillas, warmed (2 small corn tortillas per person)
Toppings such as sour cream, extra cilantro, salsa, lime wedges,
    cheese, avocados

## Instructions:

Place the garlic, cilantro leaves, lime juice, cumin, salt, and black pepper in a food processor, and pulse until all ingredients are roughly chopped and combined. Be sure to scrape down the sides of the bowl to combine everything.

Place the mahi mahi in a 1-gallon resealable plastic bag, and add the herb mixture. Set the fish aside to marinate at room temperature for 15 to 20 minutes.

Heat the grill to medium-high heat, and liberally coat the grates with oil. Remove the fish from the marinade (discard the marinade), and place the fish on the grill. Grill 4 minutes per side.

Place the fish in a bowl, and roughly shred it with two forks.

Add the fish to warmed tortillas (we like to throw our tortillas on the grill for a few seconds), and allow everyone to add their favorite toppings.

NOTE: You can also cook the fish on the stove by preheating a nonstick pan over medium-high heat. Add 1 tablespoon of oil, and when it begins to shimmer, add the fish. Cook for 4 to 5 minutes per side, until it easily flakes with a fork.

## TRICK

Looking for a quick yummy sauce? Take 1 cup mayonnaise or plain Greek yogurt, and add citrus and fresh herbs, like 1 tablespoon fresh lime juice and 1 teaspoon chopped, fresh cilantro. Adjust seasonings for taste (add salt if needed!). Use with veggies, burgers, and especially fish tacos.

# *eight*

## COMMUNION AT THE TABLE

*"I have earnestly desired to eat this
Passover with you before I suffer."*

LUKE 22:15

Jesus instituted communion at the table during the Passover meal as one of his last acts before his arrest. I like to imagine the disciples as they took their places for Passover—so seemingly oblivious of their need for Jesus' whole life to be poured out. They couldn't have begun to fathom *how* poured out. How Jesus needed to endure every stripe and strike so that we could know salvation.

The Jews had practiced the Passover supper for fourteen centuries by the time Jesus sat down to eat this meal. It was a ritual that commemorated God's miraculous rescue of the Jewish people out of slavery in Egypt. Every year, as the people sat down to this meal, they remembered the final meal in Egypt just before they fled—a meal of haste, as seen in the bread that didn't have time to rise or be leavened, and a meal of sacrifice, as seen in the lamb whose blood Moses instructed the people to put on the doorposts as a sign for the Lord's judgment to pass over them. The Passover became a celebration the Israelites observed annually to remember God's mighty hand of rescue: "Then Moses said to the people, 'Remember this day in which you came out from Egypt, out of the house of slavery, for by a strong hand the LORD brought you out from this place. No leavened bread shall be eaten'" (Exodus 13:3).

Years later, as Jesus invited his disciples to partake in the Passover meal with him, he did at that table what he'd been doing his whole earthly life: taking the old and making it new. He moved from Passover supper, the old meal, into the Last Supper, the new meal. He replaced the sacrificial lamb with his own body, that of the promised Savior the Jewish people had been waiting for to redeem them from the evils of this world.

He started out the evening by saying, "I have *earnestly* desired to eat this Passover with you" (Luke 22:15, emphasis mine). Earnest, with great conviction, the Savior of the world, in great anticipation, broke bread with twelve broken and worn men and let them in on the great deliverance that was about to take place. Then he revealed the transition from Passover supper to the Last Supper, saying, "This is my body, which is for you. Do this in remembrance of me. . . . This cup is the new covenant in my blood. Do this, as often as you drink it, in remembrance of me" (1 Corinthians 11:24–25).

The last command of the Savior of the world before gut-wrenching betrayal and his brutal murder was, "Remember me." For the Jewish people this request to remember was not unfamiliar. Historically, God's biggest issue with the Israelites was how they didn't remember the many ways he had worked on their behalf. The Old Testament is filled with God's exhortation for his chosen people to remember all he has done for them. And yet there are so many stories of how the people forgot the works of God and failed to follow his commands. They forgot and therefore were unable to honor God as God. So fickle were they in their forgetting that even after miracles and mighty acts of rescue from slavery in Egypt, the people failed to remember what God had done for them and turned to the worship of idols. As a result, they wandered in a desert for forty years, a desert that was only meant to be a quick path to the promised land.

So, fourteen centuries later, it seems fitting that Jesus would institute communion and say that we take of the bread and wine to *remember* him and how he redeemed us. This is the essence of the practice of communion. It's our response to our Savior's admonition to remember his blood sacrifice through a continual coming to the table, a regular partaking of the bread and the wine. It's the great act of not forgetting who saved us and who works on our behalf.

Our redemption finds its legs in our remembrance of Jesus. It is around a meal that we are able to speak redemption over ourselves by testifying and remembering what Jesus did for us. Our communion today looks very different from the Last Supper. Rarely have I shared the Last Supper around a table over a meal.

And then there was Australia. There, my view of when and how to take communion was forever changed.

I don't always camp, but when I do I make sure I am in a rainforest in Australia. Unfortunately. After I graduated college, I felt restless and wild. I had a job at a marketing firm, but I could barely breathe through the days because it was such a demanding job. I was going from being a creative, energetic young lady to being a woman well worn with the cares of this world. I was dimming, so I quit and signed up to do a six-month stint with Youth with a

Mission (YWAM) in Australia. Part of that commitment included two weeks of camping. I must have completely skipped over this requirement or had a bout of blindness when reading everything this mission consisted of. But there I was that October, in Australia with my team, loaded into buses and then dropped off in the middle of nowhere.

We marched to different areas of the rainforest and received instructions about where to set up camp. After numerous tries wrestling with my tent unsuccessfully, I took a deep breath in complete frustration and looked up, hoping for a sign of peace. Instead of receiving reassurance that God hadn't left me alone, I saw one very large black snake coiling around a tree. This, my friends, is the opposite of peace for me. This is the height of me needing the laying on of hands and the strong prayers of the saints.

The thing about the rainforest is, you can't not be under trees. And rainforest trees are large, and their branches reach out into the branches of other trees, creating a web so one can barely see the sky. And with these large, interwoven rainforest trees come snakes. In sheer panic, I stepped backward, almost knocking into a girl standing behind me with her camera TAKING PICTURES. I wanted to remind her that the only appropriate response to spotting a big black snake is to run.

She looked at me and said, with effortless fascination, "Cool, huh?"

I darted a look at her that I'm sure conveyed, "Totally cool! Death. By. Snake. I mean, amazing, right?!" Moments later, the whole team gathered together to go over ground rules. The following is an accurate depiction of what I heard from our leader:

"Okay, everybody, we're here for fourteen days. This is a real rainforest filled with real animals that are very dangerous, but if we're careful we will all be safe. First off, snakes. Most of them are poisonous, but they like to be in the trees, so just let them be.

Kangaroos can kill you with one kick. If you see one, stay still. Do not run. Do not move. It will lose interest and move on. Also, there is a leaf in this forest that causes paralysis, so please do not brush up against it. Most of the spiders are poisonous, so make sure to shake out your sleeping bag real good before going to bed."

After this important public service announcement, we ended in prayer, but I am not sure what the leader said because I kept whispering, "Jesus, please don't let me die. Please don't let me die. Please don't let me die."

The next fourteen days were some of the most dangerous days of my life. Half of our team had ticks dig into their bodies throughout those two weeks. Thankfully, to my knowledge, no one became paralyzed. One night, while walking back to my tent, my tent mates and I could feel the ground moving—*Jurassic Park* style. Once we reached our tent, one of my friends focused her headlamp directly in front of us, only to reveal a kangaroo. I had never stood so still in all my life, which must have suited the kangaroo because he (or she?) continued right along. A few nights later we arrived at our tent to find one massive spider on our tent door, *eyeing* my sleeping bag! We took this very seriously and used what we had on hand (my hair spray) to kill the spider. Why I had hairspray in the rainforest is a topic for a completely different kind of book; I will just remind you that I had rarely camped at this point in my life. But I'm not even embarrassed about it because my hairspray saved our lives. Hairspray, adding body to hair and protecting women since 1602. Or something like that.

Even though those fourteen days were full of the kind of adventure I didn't really appreciate, there were breathtaking moments too, like nights filled with so many stars I felt like it was the first time I was really seeing the night sky. I also grew close with four other girls—the same girls I see every year now for an annual girls' trip. The quietest moments I have ever shared with God happened in that forest, and there were times I could almost feel him breathing on me.

The last afternoon of that trip was one I will never forget for the rest of my life. Because, cyclone. Our whole team had gathered in a circle to share stories and praise. It was a bright day with barely any clouds. But, then again, the web of branches above us was hard to see through. About thirty minutes into sharing, I felt a large gust of wind move right through us. I looked up and saw the branches of trees impossibly untangle and part. The wind had moved so furiously that the branches bent backward and made a clearing for us to see the sky. This all seemed to happen in slow motion, and my lips parted as I just as slowly whispered, "Wow."

Moments later, a torrential downpour of rain started falling on us, and the wind raged harder. Our group ran in all directions, unsure about where to go. Trees fell to the ground all around us. At one point, I stepped out to move to a clearing when my friend Donavan grabbed my hand and pulled me into him right as a tree fell where I had just moments before been standing. Our leaders eventually corralled all of us into the concrete room where we kept our food and instructed us to grab a buddy and run for the entrance of the forest. We would find safety at the dirt road.

Our leaders went first, guiding us through fallen trees. The floodwater was up to our shins and continuing to rise. Up ahead, some of the guys had been stationed on the path where some larger trees had fallen so they could help the girls up and over. We ran quickly, strategically moving past branches, watching spiders and snakes being carried away by the rushing water. We were fearless. Finally, we made it to the entrance of the forest, only to discover that it was blocked by trees—there was no hope to climb out. At that moment, the wind dissipated and the rain stopped. We watched as the pool of water nearing our knees started to recede.

After a while, we moved gingerly back to our campsite. No

one, not one person, had been hurt. Not even a scratch. We stayed still, like we knew we were on holy ground, while our leaders accounted for all of us. Our adrenaline, which had kept us moving in the waters filled with floating creatures, started to deplete. We also began noticing our almost immediate and intense hunger.

A few of us went to the stock room and found all the food destroyed except for biscuits and grape juice, so we turned over a table and laid out the elements. We didn't sit around the table so much as we huddled in. We needed to be impossibly close to one another. One of our leaders prayed, then we reached out our hands to grab biscuits and juice. Everyone was quiet, understanding that what we had just witnessed pointed directly to the awesome power of God. The biscuit crumbling in our mouths gave us a visceral appreciation as we remembered Jesus and what he is capable of. We brushed crumbs from our lips with our soggy shirtsleeves and gulped juice to relieve our thirst. Finally, someone broke the silence with the only thing that made sense, blasting U2's song "Beautiful Day" over a still-working speaker.

We grabbed hands with the people next to us and danced and drank more juice, crying out, "It's a beautiful day!" This was the kind of communion I longed for. The kind that hushes us as we remember who God is and what he has done. *He is mighty. He is mighty to save.* The kind of communion that doesn't just make us solemn but releases within us an urge to dance. *We were lost, but now we're found.* It's the ability to take whatever we have before us (even if it is just biscuits and juice) and break it and, by doing so, join in Christ's broken body for us. And then be filled with hope as we hear his words echo in our soul, "I will come and eat with you again."

Before receiving communion in the rainforest, I had always received communion solely in church. And, even though I have attended many churches in many states, it always looked fairly the same. The congregation received the bread and juice, then we had a few moments of silence to confess and remember and eat. I'm assuming this is like most of your communion experiences as well, but if we look carefully at how Jesus modeled it for us, how he reclined at a table with his closest people in an intimate room, today's communion seems to stand in stark contrast. How do we create a place for intimate communion in our own homes, reclined at the table, the way Jesus first instituted it?

First, we need to start with the question, "Why do we take communion?" Answering this question moved me closer to bringing communion into my home and increased how often I participated in this breaking. I take communion because I am desperate to remember what Christ did for me. I cannot go one day, let alone one hour, without continuing to pull his sacrificial death down into my own life.

We remember because without recalling what Jesus did for us, we become as the Israelites once were, wandering a dusty desert of despair. If we will not become remembering people, we will become wandering people. We remember because our flesh is crushing us and telling us we got it wrong, we should tap out, we should spend more, buy more, judge more, compare more. The practice of communion is like an anchor for our souls as they are being tossed in tumultuous seas. If we can bring this practice into our very own homes, to our very own tables, what might our lives look like? Could it mean more joy? More grace? More gratitude?

In light of this, Jeremy and I started to reinvent how and where we take communion. We still enjoyed communion in the church, but we needed a little bit more. More time. More remembering. So now we take communion in our home, at our table. It's not traditional. It's not always a sip of wine and the breaking of unleavened bread. It's whatever food and drink we have before us, which might feel kind of odd when we're having, say, burgers and sparkling water, but in its simplest form, communion is a ceremony that leads us to remembering that Jesus died for us, that he took our place on the cross to give us peace with God. We do this by sharing our thankfulness and our commemoration of the Lord.

**TIP:** A great practice to usher communion into your time at the table is to read some of your favorite Bible verses. Begin by going around the table and letting each person read a verse he or she loves. Then move into a time of communion.

For Jeremy and me, taking communion at home has been completely organic. It's not a to-do for our mealtimes. We rely on the prompting of the Holy Spirit. We have taken it during joyous times and in the middle of mundane weeks. Most recently we took communion after I had walked through a heart-shattering decision. I was standing, quite awkward and small, at our counter as Jeremy and I made homemade pizza. I had already cried three times that day, so I was hoping to keep it together for the remainder of the night. But while we were waiting for the dough to bake, Jeremy asked, "So, how are you?"

I put my hand out as if to signal him to stop. "Please don't . . ." and the tears came again.

He pulled me in and said, "Hey, I am the safe place."

In between choking sobs, I listed off everything that was crushing me. I recounted all my fears clearly and carefully, because it was the last time I wanted to visit those fears.

We pulled the pizza from the oven and cut our slices. We served up glasses of wine, and I let the red liquid poured out remind me of Jesus.

We weren't even sitting at our table. We were sitting on the couch because Friday nights are our designated movie and pizza nights. We were reclining when the words came.

"Hey, can we take communion?" I asked.

We brought our glasses to our lips, and I said quietly and reverently, "Jesus, I remember you. I remember everything you did for me. I'm broken and emptied, but I remember you. And how you love. I don't want to be anywhere apart from you."

Then we broke off a piece of our pizza crust, and I continued, "Thank you for remembering me too."

This is the great remembering I needed that night and most nights. It wasn't a fancy or stuffy ritual. It was my whole being aching for peace during a difficult time. It was my soul crying out, *Let's remember Jesus and what he did for us and how he loves us and is with us still today. Let's remember Jesus, because he never stopped remembering us.*

There is this great metaphor that I love to tell at my table with my people when we take communion. It's about fire. Did you know that if you are caught up in a wildfire the safest place for you to go is where the fire has already burned? Fire does not return to the area it has already raged through. This is a technique used by firemen who fight forest fires. This is also a powerful image for me as I take communion, because through it I remember the work of Jesus. I remember that all of God's wrath toward sin, my sin, was directed onto Jesus on the cross. We stand behind where the fire has already gone. We stand behind the cross. Thus we can come confidently to the throne and find forgiveness, restoration, and peace. And that's what communion at our tables allows us to remember. Why would I not want to soak my own home, my own table, in this ritual?

## PRAYER FOR THE TABLE

*Jesus, thank you for your sacrifice. Thank you that you modeled a way for us to remember what you did for us. A way to remember that there is now no condemnation for us in you. Holy Spirit, grant us wisdom as we desire to participate in a communion that is holy and unrushed. May we be part of many little rehearsals before the grand marriage banquet.*

## QUESTIONS FOR THE TABLE

1. One unique way of bringing communion to your table is to take some time to share your testimony over a meal. If you've already shared it with your people, find a creative way to share it again. Try doing it in new and varied ways: in three sentences or less, only using verbs, or even in a riddle or a haiku. This is your personal great remembering of how Jesus saved you.
2. What is a favorite memory you have of taking communion? Why was it so special?
3. What are your thoughts about taking communion inside your home with your people? If you are interested, plan a time and date to perform this ritual for the first time.

## RECIPE FOR THE TABLE

### THIN CRUST PIZZA

*This is the pizza recipe Jeremy and I made in the communion story I shared. It's quite fitting for communion because it's a grain-free dough—so it's unleavened. We have made this pizza for extreme pizza lovers, and though it is more of a thin-crust style, people of all crust preferences have loved it!*

## Ingredients:
1 cup tapioca flour
1/4 cup potato flour

1 teaspoon dried Italian herbs

1/4 teaspoon garlic powder

1/4 cup grated Parmesan cheese (optional)

1/3 cup water

1 teaspoon powdered unflavored gelatin

1 egg

1/4 cup extra-virgin olive oil

1 tablespoon harissa oil or 1/4 teaspoon crushed red pepper (optional)

1 tablespoon melted butter (optional)

Sprinkle of fleur de sel (optional)

Toppings such as pizza sauce, mozzarella cheese, pepperoni, bell peppers, red onions

## Instructions:

Preheat the oven to 400 degrees. Place a 13-inch pizza stone or large cast-iron skillet in the oven to preheat.

In a large bowl mix together the tapioca flour, potato flour, dried Italian herbs, garlic powder, and Parmesan cheese, if using.

In a small bowl add the water, and sprinkle the gelatin over the water. Add the egg and oils, and whisk to combine.

Add the egg mixture to the flour mixture and mix together (I use my hands for this part). A dough should start to form. If the dough is too dry, add water by the teaspoon. The dough should hold together but not be sticky. Keep the dough in the bowl until the pizza stone is ready.

Take the pizza stone out of the oven. Place the dough on the pizza stone, and roll it out to 1/4-inch thickness and about 10 inches in diameter. Be careful, as the stone will be hot! Remember that this is not regular pizza dough. The first few times we made this we did not get it into a perfect circle, but that is okay!

If desired, brush melted butter on the edges of the dough, and sprinkle with fleur de sel.

Bake the dough for 15 to 20 minutes, until it's golden brown around the edges.

Remove the pizza crust from the oven, and coat with pizza sauce and desired toppings. Put the pizza back in the oven for another 15 to 20 minutes until the cheese is melted.

Remove the pizza. Enjoy!

To see pictures of this recipe, visit http://oursavorylife.com/ homemade-paleo-pizza-crust/.

## TRICK

Infused garlic oil is fun to have on hand for pizza nights! It's quick and easy to make. Place 6 cloves of peeled and smashed garlic in a saucepan. Add 1 tablespoon of oil, and let cook for 3 minutes, stirring occasionally, over low heat. Add an additional 1 cup of oil, and let simmer for 5 minutes. Strain, and pour the oil into an airtight jar to use later on pastas and pizzas.

# nine

## MEEKNESS AT THE TABLE

*God has work that has to be done in work
clothes, not in one's Sunday best.*

—CHRISTOPH FRIEDRICH BLUMHARDT

This world—I'd been looking at it all wrong. In my youth, it had cooed, "Bri! You're number one! And I can help you stay there. You just need to look out for yourself. We're going to make you something really special." And because it seemed nice enough, I took a hit of what it offered. First it was popularity, which has taken me approximately my whole life to come down from. Then it let me sample pride, possessions, and power. It was all so strong. It was all so intoxicating. I got lost in the pursuit of me. This world, spinning me around until I was too dizzy to look straight, told me, "I'm all yours, baby. Live it up."

But then, while I was in my reeling stupor, the Savior of this world grabbed me by the shoulders. He called my name. And I became, with great resolve, wholly his. The aroma of his love exposed the stench of this earth, which smells like rot. God set me straight and showed me how truly twisted the economy of this world is. This world taught me to become so focused on myself that others became mere side characters in my own embellished story. I rarely encountered the poor, the lonely, or the hurting because I did not want them living in my well-to-do story.

But this Jesus way, this light-of-the-hurting-world way, was so inside out. It was so fantastically right. It went something more like this: "Lose your life to go save many others." This path the creator of the universe took? He went into the homes of the most ordinary, the most rejected, the most overlooked, and he ate with them. If there is anyone who had the right to come to this earth in grand fashion and overturn kingdoms, displace rulers, and conquer the land, it was Jesus. But he took a quieter way. A way that put his focus on others rather than on his own glory. He pulled out a chair, placed a napkin on his lap, and said, "Pass the veggies, please." Maybe our way should follow suit? Maybe we can take Jesus at his word when he said the very people who will inherit the world will be the people who reject the current self-focused way of this world: "Blessed are the meek, for they shall inherit the earth" (Matthew 5:5).

The word *meek* in this verse comes from the Greek word *praeis* and is most often referred to as humility or mildness. In its purest form, meekness, as Jesus modeled it, is having the power to do something but refraining for the preference of others:

> Have this mind among yourselves, which is yours in Christ Jesus, who, though he was in the form of God, *did not count equality with God a thing to be grasped*, but emptied himself, by taking the form of a servant, being born in the likeness of

men. And being found in human form, he humbled himself by becoming obedient to the point of death, even death on a cross. (Philippians 2:5–8, emphasis mine)

Do we take the form of a servant when we come to the table? Do we get quiet in spirit so that the people at our table can be fully seen? A table illuminated with meekness is the most piercing of all. A humbled and meek table shows up unadorned because the people at the table are the treasure. Though our guests might have come to see us, a table laid with meekness says, "I am nothing; you are the guest of honor." Meekness at the table pulls out a seat for the exiled, the weary, the poor, and proclaims, "It is my joy to eat with you, not my burden." We embody the very beating life of Jesus when we choose to stoop low in service of others. We put away our fancy frills and put on our let's-go-to-work attire.

Meekness has been a hard concept for me to pull into my life. For a long time, I tried to reconcile how my personality intersected with meekness. I can be loud, and I tip the scales on extroversion. I have a story for every topic, and I want to wildly engage with everyone else's story. On the surface the concept of getting quieter in spirit so that others can be more fully seen can seem extra difficult for someone like me. But meekness does not require a change of personality; it requires a change of perspective.

Jesus had amazing stories; he had searing truths. People asked him questions ad nauseum. He often became the center of attention at meals. At first glance, this may not seem to fit our ideas about what it looks like to be meek. But perhaps meekness is more about emptying ourselves for the sake of others and less about having to do this in a way that fits only one personality. Jesus embodied humility and still told his stories. He still commanded a room. He still healed the sick and called out to the lonely. And people were drawn to his compassion, his way of focusing on them and peering deep into their hearts. In the end, what was so powerful was the intention behind his actions, the way everything he did spoke to his heart for them. This approach, this spirit, is in direct opposition to the way of the world, and a table etched with Jesus' meekness chooses this same way. In following him, we choose service, not status. Humility, not dripping symbols of pride.

Sometimes, having a spirit of meekness at the table means purposefully laying down your own concerns and looking to engage in the hurt of the world. When I was in college, I had a group of friends who were committed to learning more about the pain of the world so we could know where to shine our light. Though we were all born middle class, we did not count it as an excuse, or our privilege, to shield ourselves from the rest of the hurting world. So we explored the darkest caves. No land was off-limits. We did this by picking a book every month that dealt with social justice issues. We would read it and then come together over a meal—a meal we prepared with food from the land we were learning about. As we shared food that was new to us, we would discuss the book, share ideas on how we could help, and sometimes sit in silence with forks in hand, stewing on our thoughts about how our big God could use our little sacrifice of learning and donating and sharing. In a world that is teeming with evil and shattered lives, we took what little steps we had to offer at that table in our friends' homes.

One evening we decided to watch a documentary about a jungle buried in the heart of the Congo. We spooned out African dishes we had learned to make and took our places on the couch. The guy who brought the video queued it up and whispered with caution, "Hey, guys, this is . . . this is going to be heavy." We all nodded in solemn reply. You know, the "we're all in" nod. The "we don't want to choose ignorance" nod.

As we watched we learned that women were being savagely raped by men anytime they went into this jungle to get wood. It was not an "if" situation. It was "when." Many of the women would wait until their children were to the point of starvation before they finally made another journey into the jungle. They needed wood for fire to cook food. To boil water. To heat their huts. And so they went, each one carrying as much back as they could, always returning home brutalized.

That night I felt this strange tear in my heart. It felt like burning. It felt impossible to bear. In complete shock to myself, I yelped out a sound that resembled what a hurt animal might make. My friends, all of them already tearstained, looked up at me, and I pleaded, "Stop." We turned the video off, and in unison we fell to the ground in prayers and heaving tears unfamiliar to us. I wept in a way I had never experienced. It felt like I was holding the fear and the pain of these sisters I had never met. Eventually we all hushed, and we sat like statues made timid by our own cracking sobs. We shyly admitted, "I've never cried like that before." And then my girl Ashlee named it. "It sounded like God."

We finished the video, because these women could not afford for us to look away. At the end was a plethora of information on how we could help. We all scribbled fast, and our broken hearts accepted hope as we entered into compassion for the hurting. We all left that night painfully exhausted. You know the kind of exhausted you feel after crying for hours? The kind of empty you feel after walking into complicated matters with not even one answer. But for weeks to come, we each acted on this new knowledge in our own ways, looking for opportunities to engage. And all because that night, over food from a different land, we had sojourned together into the hurt of an African village. We had poured ourselves out by choosing to set aside our own concerns for a night to learn about hurting places holding hurting people. We had been called by God to our knees and had interceded for women we'd never met. We kept ourselves open, journeying into the dark, assured of the light we had to shine. Assured that we were put on this earth to stoop low, not to climb ladders of praise or self-fullfillment.

You and I have got work to do around our tables, haven't we? We've got ourselves to pour out, to offer without a second thought to the people God brings to us. Jesus' meekness was displayed through his ultimate and final act on the cross, when he did not spare even one drop of blood to save humanity. And isn't this how God calls us? He calls us to lay down our lives. Despite our privilege or our zip code. It's just like how he called Joseph or Noah. Moses and David. Esther and Mary. Each of them with varying degrees of status or power, but each with lives all used up and wrung out to save other lives.

Jesus' time on this earth was the prime example of a life thoroughly used by God, of what it looks like to be wholly employed by God for his work. This pouring out, this putting the needs of others above ourselves, this losing our lives so others can taste and see that God is good—it must be practiced at our tables. Isn't this the place we show up to most often anyway? We are already there; we just need to take another step to meet God where we already are, emptying and pouring ourselves out in humility. With relentless intention, we must choose not to esteem or puff ourselves up in the eyes of others. In spirit we must crouch lower and lower and lower, making room for the other hearts at the table. Although we are made in the likeness of God, we must choose to serve and to use our lives as an arrow to point to him. Over and over again.

Pouring myself out at my table these days rarely looks like that table I sat at in college, the communal lament for the heartaches of a far-away people. Most nights it looks more like me taking the humble position Jesus did with the person sitting right in front of me. It looks like me intentionally stepping away from the preoccupation of my own insular concerns and instead looking to wholeheartedly engage with the need Jesus has brought to my table. My friend Edie often reminds her people of a quote from Pauline Phillips, journalist and creator of the Dear Abby column in 1956: "There are two kinds of people in the world. Those who walk into a room and say, 'There you are' and those who say, 'Here I am.'"[1] This is the best and most concise explanation I know for the heart behind a table laid with meekness. It seeks out the other. It proclaims, "I want *you* to be fully seen, and for that, I am in service to you." The way of meekness puts little value on our own matters and intrinsic value on the people right in front of us.

Are we "there you are" people at our tables? Do we value meekness? Do we come to a place where we plead with God, "Use me up, reclaim every drop of my life, if only to redeem every drop of another soul"? We can come like he did, eating and drinking and fully awake to the person in front of us. We can, with our bright lives, be depleted unendingly at the table for those who surround us. We can proclaim with our lives what Francis of Assisi laid out in words: "Remember that when you leave this earth, you take with you nothing that you received—fading symbols of honor, trappings of power—but only what you have given; a full heart enriched by *honest service, love, sacrifice, and courage*" (emphasis mine).[2]

This way of humility, this way of allowing God to use every drop of us, every day, in service to others, is the kind of dying to

> **TIP:** Meekness is not a change of personality; it is a change of perspective. Take time this week to thank God for the unique way he created you, and let him speak to you about how you can walk in meekness according to his design.

self Jesus talks about. It's weighty and often feels just on the cusp of impossible, especially by the end of the day when we're already scraping the bottom of our cups for what's left of us. But we take heart. We must remember that the table can be a symbol, an altar of sacrifice and humility, that whatever we do have left can be spent and poured out over the last meal of the day. Humility is hard at any time of day, let alone the last hours after we've run a full race. But we can trust Jesus to miraculously use even the small drop we have left. Then we can trust as we go to bed that in the morning we will be refreshed. With new loving-kindness. Fresh mercies.

May the table be the ribbon at the finish line where we gather up our reserves and, with full gusto, complete the day as a vessel poured out, a people who did not consider our lives more worthy than the ones seated next to us. May we end each day with hands calloused from working. Hearts swollen from loving. Knees bruised from kneeling.

## PRAYER FOR THE TABLE

*Jesus, thank you for coming as you did, as a babe and then as a humble servant. Never calling on your power or position but kneeling and sacrificing. May we lean into your life and make it our own. Stir us, Holy Spirit, as we come to the table at the end of the day, to pour ourselves out in service. Use us all up, then fill us again.*

## QUESTIONS FOR THE TABLE

1. How have you seen meekness or humility practiced at the table over a meal?

2. Have you struggled with meekness? How so?

3. Is there someone in your life who embodies a "there you are" mentality? What about them communicates that they are more about others than themselves?

4. What is one thing you can change at your table to consistently practice humility?

## RECIPE FOR THE TABLE

## WHITE CHICKEN CHILI

Serves 5 to 6.

*This soup is packed with flavor and extremely simple to make, so no unnecessarily complicated instructions here. You can use leftover chicken or buy a rotisserie chicken and just pull the meat off the bones (you can freeze the leftover meat for up to one month). This recipe helps us get to the table quicker so we can focus more on serving the people at our table, not just serving a meal.*

## Ingredients:

1 tablespoon coconut oil

1 medium onion, chopped

2 cups shredded cooked chicken

1 1/2 teaspoons garlic powder

2 1/4 cups chicken broth, divided

1 (15.5-ounce) can Great Northern beans, rinsed and drained

1 cup frozen corn (optional)

4 ounces fresh roasted and chopped green chiles (or one 4-ounce can chopped green chiles)

1 teaspoon salt

1 teaspoon ground cumin

1 teaspoon dried oregano

1/2 teaspoon black pepper

1/4 teaspoon cayenne pepper

1 cup plain Greek yogurt (optional)

1/2 cup heavy whipping cream (optional)

## Instructions:

Heat a large pot or Dutch oven over medium heat. Add the coconut oil, and allow it to melt. Add the onion, and cook until translucent, stirring occasionally, about 3 minutes.

Add the shredded chicken and garlic powder, and stir to combine. Pour in 1/4 cup of the chicken broth and stir, scraping the bottom of the pot to loosen any browned bits. Cook for 2 minutes.

Add the remaining 2 cups chicken broth, beans, corn, chiles, salt, cumin, oregano, and black and cayenne peppers. Turn the heat to high, and bring to a boil. Then reduce the heat to medium-low and simmer, uncovered, for 30 minutes.

Taste the soup, and add additional salt or pepper if needed. The soup may be served like this, or for a super creamy chili, remove the pot from the heat, and stir in the Greek yogurt and cream. Serve warm.

To learn how to make batches of your own roasted green chiles (which will last in the freezer for up to three months), visit http://oursavorylife.com/substitute-for-canned-green-chilies/.

For step-by-step pictures of this recipe, visit http://oursavorylife.com/white-chicken-chili-recipe-2/.

## TRICK

If you cook chicken breasts to shred for your meal, forget shredding them by hand! Cut your cooked chicken breasts in half, and throw them into the bowl of a stand mixer. Attach the paddle attachment and turn the mixer on, slowly increasing the speed. You'll have pounds of shredded chicken in minutes.

## *ten*

# STORY AT THE TABLE

*And He began speaking a parable*
*to the invited guests . . .*

LUKE 14:7 NASB

My great-grandmother's trailer sits in a cloudy haze in my memories. If I reach too hard for it, it all seems to dissipate, so I try to keep it preserved by infrequent visits. When I do visit, I recreate the drive into the middle of what seemed to be nowhere. There was a river. Lots of green grass and trees and bumblebees and lightning bugs. Every time we stepped out of our van, I'd immediately feel sticky from the humidity. It wrapped me like a blanket, like a true and thorough greeting. The air always swooned balmy with cut grass and morning dew, and I could be sure that by the time we left in the evening I'd be covered in grass stains, probably have a bee sting or two, and be full up on delicious home-made biscuits and gravy.

The other thing I knew I'd leave full of was story. Whenever we got together at great-grandma's trailer, we'd spend a good amount of time just talking around the kitchen table. The chatter of my family filled the space of that table like it was a record playing. Stories from the day's happenings and years gone by dripped from our mouths, and right there, as far back as I can remember, I started to learn the art of storytelling. I started to learn that we bring dishes to the table. We bring ourselves. And we graciously bring our stories.

Those evenings at my great-grandma's weren't fancy by any means, but they were holy. The kitchen was impossibly small, but the dining room table looms large in my mind. I remember sitting down to that big, long table in my great-grandma's tiny trailer and seeing the spread. We barely had enough room for our plates. Being as tiny as I was, I couldn't eat much food, so I always had to take a careful inventory and then slowly eliminate dishes from my mind's menu to retain room in my stomach for the most spectacular options. Once I had made my mental selections I'd pass my plate, and my parents would scoop out some of the best food I'd ever eaten.

"Do you want biscuits and gravy, Bri baby?" my mom would ask. She was always trying to fill my plate with as much food as she could.

"Just half a biscuit, please, and a little gravy. I want to make room for the sour cream salad. And lots of green beans, please!"

Once my plate was full, I'd tuck in and listen to the adults as they talked and laughed. Sometimes, after maybe an hour, my cousins would get restless and excuse themselves to go back out and play. But not me. I'd offer my services for any task just so I could stay with the adults a little longer. I'd be hard focused and stay real quiet so they wouldn't ask me to go out and play with the cousins while they talked about grown-up things. When washing the dishes, I'd turn the faucet down low so I could hear Grandma and Mom tell stories, like the one about when the cows got outside the gate early one morning and how my aunt, though barely taller than five feet, carried out a triumphant rescue, scaling the hills in the still pitch-dark morning and herding every single cow back into the pasture.

My family knew how to take the events of the day and weave them into stories that had everyone by turns laughing and stunned silent in shock. That table was a world that was always inviting, full of a continual stream of shared memories, more recent adventures, and truths that transcended whatever era the stories originated in. I felt safe and immensely loved getting to listen in on those lazy afternoons. My love for the kitchen and the fellowship around the table started then, though I wouldn't realize it fully for twenty more years.

If there's one thing that makes me feel deeply connected to the kitchen and the power of a shared table today, it's scrolling through memories of my great-grandma's, grandma's, and mother's kitchens and recalling the stories they told in those spaces. I'm grateful for those summers when I got to simply be in the kitchen with the women in my family, quietly observing, listening to them talk and laugh and be family, seeing firsthand the power of gathering and sharing stories around the table. Even though my great-grandma is gone now, those moments and the chatter of voices at her table penetrate my being, and like a time capsule I gently and reverently hold their stories.

Jesus was the best storyteller. He answered most people's questions in story form, using metaphors and colorful examples. I think he knew just how much everyone loved a good story and how narratives have the inexplicable ability to employ emotion and fact in a way that causes us to not only understand the purpose in a palpable way but to also remember that story for years to come. In a way, we're all storytellers, aren't we? I didn't always think this. When I was in college, I was surrounded by some amazing friends who could weave a story like they were breathing air. Effortless. Intuitive. They entered story slams and recited poetry smoothly while sharing the events of their day. That was my idea of a storyteller. But then I learned the true art of telling a story: showing up to my own life. Aren't we every day living out the stories of our lives, bumping up against one another's stories in our every step or decision? When we take a moment to think about this, the everyday happenings and God's work in the midst of them, suddenly we all have stories to tell at the end of the day—stories that just might speak exactly to whatever someone sitting at our table is needing to hear. The key to becoming a storyteller at our tables is paying attention to the stories we're living before we even arrive.

There is a ministry in being vigilant with our one sacred life, and it starts with being interested and curious. My life is consumed with mostly mundane hours and errands and the needs of my family. It's easy to check out and just coast. But if I want to be intentional about telling the stories God is giving me when I come to the table, I must feel an urgency to open my eyes even to the routine of my daytime hours. As John Piper tells us, "God is always doing 10,000 things in your life, and you may be aware of three of them."[1] God uses us in ways we are scarcely aware of, but we can show up more purposefully every morning and whisper to Jesus, "I want to be awake to the stories you are writing in my life today. I want to lean less into the random and more into the divinely orchestrated." Jesus loves these prayers; he knows that we cannot do hard things on our own, but with him we can do holy things.

The great thing about choosing to be attentive is that even though we might miss our cue (a lot)—and even sometimes the curtain call—God is so amazing at nudging us. I believe if we come to him every morning and say things like, "Hi! Here I am!" and, "You put me here, so I want to be present in this day, not just be part of the day," and, "Lord, please let me be part of what you're doing today," then I think he will start to peel the film of complacency from our eyes, and we will see glimpses of his hand and actions in our everyday lives.

Our presence at any table is a direct reflection of the living we did during the day. If we pay attention, we get to enter other people's stories every day. We get to speak life with a smile or a kind word or an act of service. And that's it. We're in. They're living in our story, and we're in theirs. Then we get to take it to the table. To our people. We get to show up at the end of the day and say, "I was living today, and God put this person in front of me and we entered each other's stories. And here is what God did." I know this because of a mom at Target.

Yesterday I was at Target because we were out of toilet paper. I get my toilet paper at Target because it means I get to make a trip to Target! It did not occur to me that Target on a Friday morning is a mecca for all mothers with toddlers. The store was packed, so I quickly grabbed my needed items and a few, "Oh yeah, I probably definitely need this" items and went through the checkout. After checking out I noticed how congested the path to the exit doors was and had to wait for an opening so I could fit myself and my cart down the walkway.

After a little while, I finally noticed a clearing and made my move, but as I pulled into the flow I noticed a mother directly in front of me had also seen the clearing and was making her move too. Of course I waved the mother onward, because mothers are heroes as we all know. So, obviously, she gets to go first! She was pushing her cart a little awkwardly and moving quite slowly. She kept glancing up at me with this worried, "I'm sorry. I'm sorry. I'm so sorry!" look on her face. I immediately recognized that look because I give it all the time myself. I give that look whenever I feel that I am an inconvenience to someone. I suffer from "I care a lot about what other people think" syndrome. But the Holy Spirit was paying attention, and he whispered, *Bri, wake up. That mom needs encouragement.*

Because I am learning to pay attention to how God made me, I knew exactly what to do. I gave her one of my big Bri smiles and a reassuring head nod. You know, the "Carry on!" head nod. The "I'm not annoyed. No worries!" head nod. Something amazing happened once she saw this: her whole demeanor softened. She stopped rushing her little girl along, the one who it turned out was pushing the cart, and became gentler toward her. As she passed she gave me a nod back. You know, the "Thanks! Very grateful!" head nod. Because we were paying attention to each other, we were able to live more fully in that moment. And I carried that story with me all day right to the dinner table.

Bringing these daily stories to the table is so important because

> **TIP:** A fun activity to encourage storytelling at the table is to give each person a piece of paper at the beginning of the meal. Allow everyone five minutes to create a drawing. At the end of the five minutes, everyone passes their drawing to the person on their left, and then that person has to tell a story that goes along with the drawing. You can learn a lot about each other this way, and it might even lead to some real-life stories!

it's a reminder at the end of the day that we showed up. It's a sharpening to those at our table, making them think about whether they are showing up too. Instead of responding to the worn-out dinner-time question, "How was your day?" with, "It was fine," we can answer with, "Today God showed me some of the work he is doing around me. I was paying attention, and he invited me to be a part of the story he is writing!"

When I shared the story of the mom at Target with some of my friends at the table, one gal said, "I want to show up like that too." And the very next week, we were back at the table, and she was sharing stories of how she had chosen to live more attentively as well. Her stories encouraged me to keep showing up too. It became this beautiful cycle of, "Okay, I'm going to live fully today, and I'm going to carry those stories to the table. And then I'm going to listen to the stories from my people and be likewise encouraged, sharpened, and amazed."

When I think of the ministry God does through the telling of stories, I always think of one experience in particular. Right after our honeymoon Jeremy and I moved to Florida. I didn't know anyone in Florida at the time, and I would come to learn that if there is one thing the first months of marriage needs, it's community. We walked into our tiny apartment and a few days later walked into the church down the street. We visited on the perfect day, because at the end of the service the leaders of community groups were available to talk to anyone interested in joining. Jesus is all about timing.

Jeremy headed to the meeting area while I made a quick detour to the bathroom. When I arrived to join Jeremy afterward, I noticed him talking quite a bit and rather enjoyably with a guy I had not met. Because Jeremy had already lived in Florida for two years, I assumed it was someone he knew, but it turned out Garrett Knowlan had just walked right up to Jeremy and introduced himself.

Garrett, who was also in the military, and his wife, Meg, turned out to be the brightest gifts from God to our first year of marriage. When we found out they loved food and Jesus, we were hooked. It took barely a few conversations before we felt completely safe telling them everything, and I mean everything, that went down that first year. Nothing was off-limits. I don't really know how our marriage would have emerged after 365 days without them. They were a safe place and a fun place and a prayerful place.

When Jeremy was deployed one year later, Meg and Garrett's home became my healing place. I went there for meals. I went there to cry. I went there to forget and laugh. I even went there some nights to sleep. We made master plans for what the four of us would do when Jeremy returned from his deployment. Go out to our favorite restaurant—of course! Beach time—yes! Camping—probably (I had recovered from my rainforest trauma by then)! Jeremy returned in August 2012, and the plans were set: the four of us would go out to celebrate Garrett's birthday.

A few nights after Jeremy returned, we had some of his air force mates over. I planned a nice big meal with steak, mashed potatoes, roasted veggies, and a key lime pie. Everyone was mingling while snacking on some appetizers, and I stood dutifully at the stove waiting for the moment when I could start mashing the potatoes. I looked at my phone and noticed Meg had called. *I'll call her back tonight,* I thought, as I grabbed the masher. A few minutes later Jeremy came into the kitchen and touched my shoulder.

"Hey, Bri, we have to go over to Meg's house," he said slowly and quietly.

"Um, we cannot go over to Meg's house; we are about to serve a meal to your friends!" I said while waving my masher in the air and pointing to all the people in our house.

"Bri, we really need to go. Please come with me."

Still oblivious to why in the world I would leave my house filled with people ready to eat, I turned around and staked my ground. "We cannot leave, Jeremy. Invite them over here!"

"Brianne, Garrett died. We need to go now."

There is this funny thing the mind and heart do when shattering news is delivered. They take their time catching up to each other. My heart began to crack, but my mind did not understand. I stood there, cocked my head to the side, and said, "But the mashed potatoes? I can't leave the mashed potatoes." As I said this, big tears started to pool in my eyes. Jeremy took my hand, and at that moment my mind knew what my heart was cracking from. I erupted.

"Garret is not dead. Garrett is not dead. He is not dead. What? Why? No. We're going to see him this weekend. We made plans! What? No."

A good friend of ours quickly moved over to me and released the potato masher from my hand. "Hey, Bri, I'll finish up these potatoes. You can go." I looked up to notice that everyone in the room was staring at me. Jeremy guided me swiftly to the car, and I threw my head in my lap and sobbed. I found myself asking questions out loud, "What about Meg? What about Beckett? What about Levi?" This became the anthem of my heart for the next six months.

Here's the thing about being in the military: you almost never live near your family, so when a tragedy happens, you hope that your people in your town will come running. When we arrived, I thought we would be coming to a house filled with people. I assumed Meg had gotten the news earlier in the day and was reaching out to friends at this point. But then I stepped into the house and saw that we were the first responders along with the military personnel who had delivered the news.

A wife and mother who has just been told her husband is never going to walk through that door again is the most earth-shattering picture. It's visceral and incomprehensible all at once. I fell on Meg, sobbing, but quickly noticed Meg was not sobbing. She was completely numb; her mind and heart had not yet connected. How could they have? She had held on to Garrett just that morning.

The military personnel asked Meg if they were okay to leave. They could not leave her alone, which is why she'd called me. They had been waiting for me to arrive. Shortly afterward, two of her other good friends also arrived. Our husbands left Jessica and me to attend to Meg. That night I crawled into bed with Meg, and she held my hand and started to unravel. The next week was filled with lots of food and taking shifts to watch her two boys and a lot of crying and a lot of laughing and a lot of praying. Every day we came to the table, and every day we told stories of Garrett.

A week later Jeremy and I piled into our car and drove to Garrett's hometown for his funeral. People came from all over the country. The day of his funeral there were two very clear messages about Garrett: he was deeply in love with God and he was deeply in love with God's people. He never knew a stranger, his family and friends would all echo. Afterward, those of us who had traveled for the funeral piled into a hotel lobby and did the best thing we knew to do: we told stories about Garrett. We told the story about how we each met Garrett. We told the story about our favorite memory with him. We told stories about all the times he was constantly pointing us to Jesus. It was the greatest and most pure offering we could present during those broken days. When we came together around a meal and shared our Garrett stories, it bound us together in a raw and enduring way. We honored a person we loved, we found solidarity in our hurting and in our hoping, and it branded on our hearts stories of Garrett that, still fresh at the time, were threatened with being forgotten.

This memory is with me always. It reminds me of the power of story and its uncanny ability to connect us to one another on a deeper level. Sharing stories at the table every evening has the monumental capability to dust off the truth that God has great purpose for our lives, even in our mundane, everyday living. Let us lean into being masters at telling the stories Jesus gave us this day. May we as eagerly invite stories from our guests right at our dinner tables, looking at our table not just as a place to gather but as a stage where stories come to life, connecting us with one another at a heart level and inspiring us to think about things differently.

## PRAYER FOR THE TABLE

*Father, thank you for life! Thank you for allowing us to live, and thank you for all the curious and wonderful and even mundane things we get to bump into every day. Help us pay attention. Help us choose to show up to what you are doing in our lives. Give us your strength and your grace to live each day awake and then to come to our tables in the evening and share the stories of all the things you did through us.*

## QUESTIONS FOR THE TABLE

1. Is your table a place for stories? Are your people encouraged in the art of storytelling around the table? What makes your table either an inviting or uninviting place for stories?
2. Share one interesting story from your day. Make sure to tell it in story form. You are a storyteller. Transport the people around your table to the story you are sharing using imagery and sights and smells and even different inflections in your voice.

3. How can you encourage more stories around your table? Maybe on Thursday nights you can have a story slam, where everyone gets five minutes to share a story and vote anonymously (maybe on pieces of paper placed in a hat) on their favorite story.

## RECIPE FOR THE TABLE

## A PALEO BREAKFAST RECIPE: SWEET POTATO HASH

**Serves 4.**

*In loving memory of my great-grandma Smith, the person I most loved eating breakfast with, whose stories at the table still echo bright, we're going to have breakfast for dinner! This breakfast scramble is one of my favorites. I especially love it because it's savory. You can serve it with eggs and bacon and even the pancakes of your liking.*

## Ingredients:
5 strips bacon
2 large sweet potatoes, scrubbed and cubed (you can leave the skin on)
1 teaspoon salt
1/4 teaspoon pepper
1/2 teaspoon onion powder
1 tablespoon coconut oil
1 red or white onion, chopped
1/2 poblano pepper, chopped
2 garlic cloves, thinly sliced
1 tablespoon olive oil
2 to 4 eggs (depending on how many people you are serving)

## Instructions:

In a cast-iron skillet or frying pan over medium-high heat, cook the bacon until crispy. Remove the bacon, and place it on a paper towel–lined plate. Pour all but 1 tablespoon of the bacon fat out of the skillet, and reduce the heat to medium.

Add the cubed sweet potatoes to the skillet. Add the salt, pepper, and onion powder, and stir to coat the potatoes. Cover the skillet, and cook for 5 minutes, without stirring, so the potatoes can caramelize. Flip the potatoes, and cover again. Cook for 5 more minutes without stirring. Flip the potatoes once more, and allow to cook for 8 more minutes uncovered. Remove the potatoes and set them aside.

Add the coconut oil to the skillet, increase the heat to medium-high, and add the onions, poblano pepper, and garlic. Cook and stir for about 3 minutes until softened. Add the sweet potatoes back to the skillet. Stir and allow the hash to cook for 2 more minutes.

Taste the sweet potatoes to make sure they are cooked through. They should be browned on the outside but pillowy in the center, firm but not crunchy. Add more salt and pepper if desired.

Place another skillet over medium-high heat, and add the olive oil. When the oil is heated, crack the eggs into the pan. Allow to cook until the whites are set but the yolks are still runny, 2 to 3 minutes. Serve the sweet potato hash with eggs and bacon.

NOTE: If you'd like to keep the dish vegetarian, skip the bacon, and add 1 tablespoon coconut oil to the skillet before you add the sweet potatoes.

For step-by-step pictures of this recipe, visit http://oursavorylife.com/paleo-breakfast-recipe-sweet-potato-hash/.

## TRICK

Bacon grease is a great way to infuse flavor when sautéing vegetables or meat. After each time you fry bacon, add the bacon grease to a glass jar and store it in the refrigerator. Anytime you want to use this grease in place of oil, remove the jar from the refrigerator and add a spoonful!

## eleven

# QUESTIONS AT THE TABLE

*Be gracious in your speech. The goal is to*
*bring out the best in others in a conversation,*
*not put them down, not cut them out.*

COLOSSIANS 4:6 THE MESSAGE

One rare morning I woke up vibrant with an idea to make muffins. I'm sure on this morning Jeremy took a knee to praise God; his prayers were finally answered. You see, unfortunately for some, like my husband, I am generally not much of a breakfast person (parents, hide your children from this paragraph). Nor am I one who gravitates toward the sweeter spectrum of flavors. Just give me coffee and Jesus, as those glittery mugs say. But this morning, for some reason, I wanted to eat breakfast—and a sweet one at that.

We stirred and poured and baked the pastry, and, ten minutes before the muffins were fully baked, we pulled them out of the oven and dusted them with sugar. We were definitely not skipping that step. After another ten minutes of baking, totaling forty-five minutes of waiting and salivating, the muffins were finished. We poured fresh cups of coffee and sunk our teeth into the still-piping-hot muffins. But then, almost simultaneously, we found ourselves at the trash can, spitting out our eager bites.

It turns out we had generously salted, not sugared, our muffins. At first we thought this could be remedied by simply taking a paper towel and dusting off the salt. But then, like characters in a deranged version of *Goldilocks and the Three Bears*, we kept tasting and responding, "Still too salty!" No amount of dusting off or partially removing the muffin top remedied the situation. The salt was still there, completely overpowering the rest of the ingredients. In sullen defeat, we severed the full muffin tops (the muffin top! The most coveted part of the muffin!). I couldn't have fathomed how powerful a few granules of salt were.

Salt is potent. It's one of the most common substances on earth, and it can't be destroyed by fire or time. The use of salt spans back to the beginning of history; interestingly, it was not just used to preserve or season food but was also an important symbol: "Sharing salt was a symbol of friendship and hospitality, and ancient conflicts concluded with a meal consisting of bread and salt as a symbol of friendship."[1]

In Leviticus, when God laid out the rules for the Israelites about offerings, he commanded that no offering should be without salt. So it seems fitting that when Jesus came and walked this earth, he also referred to salt, proclaiming a new way to think about it: "You are the salt of the earth, but if salt has lost its taste, how shall its saltiness be restored?" (Matthew 5:13).

Our lives are now the offering we give to God, and we hold within ourselves the salt. For a long time, I tried to figure out how to live a salt-drenched life. This truth Jesus left us with—"you are now salt of the earth"—feels weighty. After experiencing the power and potency of just a little bit of salt through our failed muffin attempt, I wondered if perhaps living a salty life means going a quieter way. A more understated means of influence that soaks in deep and permeates our lives, flavoring our relationships and especially the ministry of our tables. But what exactly does this look like? Practically speaking, how do we live that quieter way of being the salt of the earth? As I searched in an almost obsessive manner to make sure that I honored this role, I found this verse: "Let your speech always be gracious, seasoned with salt, so that you may know how you ought to answer each person" (Colossians 4:6).

It was as if the last puzzle piece had fallen into place and I saw the whole picture. Maybe living a life of quietly potent impact has to do with how we communicate with others. Maybe it's about the tone and environment we create and whether that invites people into a place of safety and freedom, allowing their hearts to be open to Jesus. And maybe I can bring this salty life to the table specifically by making more room for questions and unobstructed discussion. The great thing about this idea is that it directly connects to the vision Jeremy and I had cast for our table: To love so extravagantly, *they'll ask why.*

Whenever I get a bright idea of something to bring to my table, I go see how Jesus did it before I act. We always look to how Jesus carried out life so we can live the fullest life. And he definitely paved the way for how to make room for questions. Let's look at his approach to the woman at the well. You can find the story in John 4.

So he came to a town in Samaria called Sychar, near the plot of ground Jacob had given to his son Joseph. Jacob's well was there, and Jesus, tired as he was from the journey, sat down by the well. It was about noon.

When a Samaritan woman came to draw water, Jesus said to her, "Will you give me a drink?" (His disciples had gone into the town to buy food.)

The Samaritan woman said to him, "You are a Jew and I am a Samaritan woman. How can you ask me for a drink?" (For Jews do not associate with Samaritans.) (vv. 5–9 NIV)

This might not seem so revolutionary to us in modern times, but Jesus did a crazy and loving thing when he struck up a conversation with the outcast woman. In those days, men did not speak to women in public without their husbands being present, nor did Jews speak to Samaritans. But Jesus cared so deeply about this woman that he broke cultural barriers to start a conversation. His extravagant love for her caused her to start asking questions.

I love the discussion that ensued, because in the first few exchanges the woman asked three questions. In fact, all her initial responses to Jesus came in question form. Jesus simply asked for a drink, and she erupted with questions. She asked, "Why are you talking to me?" and, "Don't you know that someone like you would never talk to someone like me?" and, "How can you give me something that will always satisfy me?" and lastly, "Who are you?" Only after she voiced these questions and Jesus had a conversation with her did he reveal himself as the long-awaited Messiah.

Stunned by this revelation, she went to her village and asked one last and ultimately life-changing question, "Can this be the Christ?" If we look at Jesus' life closely, we'll see that his love usually led to questions. Some questions will change lives, and we need to give people the freedom to ask them. This is the salty life we seek to live, giving others space to talk about the things deep in their hearts and always being ready to give a response that points to the hope we hold inside. When we invite people to our tables and create obvious room for questions, people show us their hearts and we, in turn, can show them Jesus.

We dipped into this firsthand when Jeremy invited a coworker named Jeff over to dinner. Jeff was visiting from his base in Ohio and had been in a hotel room for two weeks, so Jeremy wanted to bless him with a home-cooked meal. When Jeremy called to tell me, I could barely contain my joy. I always want our table to be a place that offers a home-cooked meal to someone away from home. Also, it's pretty easy to impress someone who has been living off hotel breakfast for two weeks. We made it simple: burgers and sweet potato fries. We also fried some bacon, because everyone in the history of everyone wants to walk into a house that smells like bacon. I refuse to believe otherwise.

That evening, Jeff, Jeremy, and I stood around talking and laughing together for a while before we made it to the patio, where we ate and chatted until it was dark outside. Then we lit candles and made cappuccinos. At the end of the night, as Jeff was leaving, he thanked us so many times that I could not help but stand in awe at how God used us to provide a meal and fellowship to this young man.

One week later, Jeff was back. Again, we had a wonderful time eating together, talking, and laughing. As the evening progressed, Jeff asked, "So have you two found a church?"

The question caught us both off guard because we had not yet shared with Jeff about our faith. We told him about the different churches we had visited, then I asked, "How did you know we're Christians?" He said, "You can just tell."

The conversation continued, and he asked some hard questions. He shared his thoughts on faith and Jesus and what he had studied and what he believed. Jeremy and I were honored by his trust and openness. We were honored by his questions. We leaned into the conversation with no agenda beyond genuinely wanting to understand where he was coming from and seeking to engage him where he was. That night, after Jeff left, Jeremy and I looked at each other like we had been on holy ground. There had been no easy answers, no neatly packaged transitions, just a free discussion of our convictions and a commitment to honor each other despite our differences.

I think sometimes Christians—and I know this is often true for me—become so focused on the end result of converting someone that we miss the opportunity to make room for their questions and their wondering. We try to skip the miraculous and necessary journey of that person going from not knowing God to knowing God. We need to understand that while it is amazing to be part of someone coming to Christ, it is equally an honor to walk with them up to that point. This is what creating room for questions and honest conversation at the table looks like for us. It's gracious responses, humble listening, and room for questioning and lingering. A pinch of salt can perfectly season a whole meal; we do not need to dump the whole salt cellar on the chicken. In fact, that would destroy the meal.

Jeremy and I have extended this practice of gracious discussion at the table to ourselves. We have become people who aren't afraid to ask hard questions but always season our table with gracious speech. We wait with pregnant hope until God answers us or until he comes. We have decided to be loving with each other in our responses as both of us ask each other these questions. Right now, a lot of our questions are about this hurting world. A lot of them are about if we really understand what it means to love how Jesus needs us to love for such a time as this. A lot of them are about sacrifice and humility. If you will allow me such grace, this was a recent conversation at our table.

The shooting at a gay nightclub in Orlando had just taken place. According to authorities, it was the deadliest mass shooting recorded in the United States and the nation's worst terror attack since 9/11.[2] In the midst of this tragedy, I watched the reactions of Christians. They did not seem marked with Jesus' extravagant love. There were a lot of pastors leading the conversation with some pretty hateful words. I called a dear friend of mine who is a lesbian and asked her what her take was on the Christian response to the shooting. She told me some things she'd heard pastors saying, condoning the shooting because the club was a place of sin.

This was heartbreaking, and I actually didn't believe her at first—or maybe I didn't want to believe her. So I went home and Googled, "How are Christians responding to the shooting at the gay nightclub in Orlando?" The search results were sobering. Most of what was making the news was how we were not condemning the mass murder of human beings but were, in fact, celebrating it.[3]

This is a touchy subject, so I want to be very clear. Please stay with me. At our table I was not asking, "Is homosexuality a sin?" I was asking, as Christians, as people who claim to have received the most powerful love in the world, people who proclaim that we were saved before we even deserved to be saved, how should we respond to the murder of human beings?

A few nights later Jeremy surprised me with a reservation at my favorite seafood restaurant. We squeezed into the corner of this tiny, already packed joint and picked up our conversation. We peeled shrimp and repeated questions we had already been asking.

"How can we be a place of light and hope during this tragedy?"

"How do we convey that God's love is for all people?"

"Am I living in a way that points people to Jesus' irresistible love? Or am I living in a way that makes his love seem unbearable?"

"How can we love on our gay and lesbian friends in a way that honors God right now? Today? Tomorrow?"

We spoke in question form most of the night. We walked through our inquiries slowly, tenderly, allowing for humble pauses and grief-filled silence. At one point, I felt a tear kiss the edge of my lip and tasted its salty liquid. It was subtle and shocking. We closed our meal with one more question: "Are we living our life in a way that God can use us as salt in a broken and parched land?"

Some of the questions we had immediate answers to. Some of them we are still asking. And God is refining us and responding to us even now.

A table seasoned with room for questions brings freedom. Freedom to explore thoughts, though they might seem dark and only half thought through or even completely nonsensical. A table seasoned with humble listening and gracious responses will allow us to ask hard questions but will convey, "I am asking this question because I want to be more like Jesus." Once these questions land at our table, we can start the journey toward an answer in a safe place. This journey might take days or years, but it's necessary. These conversations should begin and thrive in the safety of our table.

> **TIP:** Keep a book on your table filled with questions or a stack of Table Topics cards. This will help get questions flowing at your table!

It's hard to sit with the weight of how our everyday tables can hold the beings that God created. We are image bearers of the living God. We are complicated and messy and creative and hope filled and doubt laden. We have hearty laughs and chilling tears. This is what our table holds, and to live well when we are at the table, room for questions is necessary.

Jeremy and I keep a small saltcellar on our table. It's a visual reminder that just a little salt goes a long way. It's a reminder that we are part of God's plan to draw others to him, but we are not the be-all and end-all for the people at our table. If we can create space for them to ask aloud what is already banging in their beings, then maybe one day they'll look up and ask, "Hey, what is this hope you always have?"

## PRAYER FOR THE TABLE

*Father, thank you for trusting us to be salt in this earth. To carry your love and your peace to everyone on our path. May we be brave enough to ask and allow room for questions at our table, finding peace and knowing that we don't need all the answers. Trusting that you can use just a little bit of our love and compassion to reveal yourself to someone.*

## QUESTIONS FOR THE TABLE

1. What do you think it means to be the salt of the earth? What does it look like to bring salt to your table?
2. Is there a question (or questions) you have been asking internally that you can share at the table? Take a moment to think about what God has been speaking to you. For example, maybe he has been teaching you more about grace, and perhaps you can ask, "Am I a grace-filled person?" or "How can I show more grace?"
3. As a family, have you come up with some safe rules at the table? For example, Jeremy and I are clear with our expectations when we want to ask a hard question. I might say, "I have a question I need to ask out loud, but I am not looking for an answer. I am

looking for you to listen and pray." This can help preempt him trying to answer me when I just need to talk.

4. How can you allow more room for questions at the table?

## RECIPE FOR THE TABLE

## THE BEST BURGER RECIPE

Serves 6.

*This is the burger recipe we made for Jeff. It's great for those moments when you invite a new person over and want a casual night where everyone's at ease and feels they can share their hearts. We served it on sweet potato buns. And, of course, added the bacon.*

### Ingredients:
2 tablespoons Worcestershire sauce
1 tablespoon extra-virgin olive oil
1 tablespoon garlic powder
1 1/2 teaspoons onion powder
1/2 teaspoon salt
1/4 teaspoon pepper
2 1/2 pounds ground chuck, 80 percent lean
2 tablespoons butter, cut into 6 cubes

### Instructions:
Preheat a grill or grill pan over medium heat.

In a medium bowl mix together the Worcestershire sauce, olive oil, garlic powder, onion powder, salt, and pepper. Add the ground chuck, and massage the spice mixture into the meat.

Form 6 tennis ball–sized balls with the meat. Create a patty by flattening the ball out with your palms.

Take a pinch of meat out of the center of each patty and place a cube of butter in the indentation (this will keep the burgers from drying out while they cook). Place the meat back on each patty, fully covering the butter.

Grill the patties for 6 minutes on the first side and 4 to 5 minutes on the second side for medium. Leave them on for an additional 2 minutes for well done.

Let the burgers rest for 5 minutes. Serve with your favorite condiments.

To see pictures of this recipe and the recipe for sweet potato buns, visit http://oursavorylife.com/the-best-burger-recipe-so-good-the-bun-gets-in-the-way/.

## TRICK

Pulling your meat out of the refrigerator at least ten minutes before cooking will allow it to come to room temperature. Meat that has come to room temperature cooks more evenly, will not stick to the pan, and stays juicy!

*twelve*

# REVOLUTION AT THE TABLE

*Jesus said…"Feed my sheep."*

JOHN 21:17

We didn't understand how to live with the tension. We went to work and went to Bible study. We showed up squeaky clean at church and raised hands high while the world burned outside. We dropped our 10 percent into the collection plate and felt little loss. We skipped over the verse that said justice for the poor is what God desires. We told ourselves the Sabbath was just meant for turning off our phones, not turning toward God. But then one day we simply couldn't ignore the pain anymore.

We woke up to reports of innocent young black men being mercilessly gunned down. We wept while watching videos of Syrian refugees fleeing for their very lives. We stood horrified as children in Aleppo were being ruthlessly bombed. We held collective breaths as a hurricane swept through Haiti, destroying already impoverished towns. We winced while hate speech flew out of people's mouths due to an election that severely divided our country. The news came fast and hard and was filled with catastrophe. Barely one story was reported before others emerged. And in all of this I wanted to look away. I wanted to lock and even deadbolt my doors. I wanted to not feel the burden of a suffering people. The refugees, the sex slaves, the child soldiers, the hungry, the cold, the lonely.

But Jesus entered our lives and called us light. And light is made to shine in the dark, not behind the safety of latched doors. We must take the pierced hands of Jesus and let him lead us right into the raw reality of this world. We must show up and ask: How do we move through this world with eyes-open compassion and a heart for real-life change the way Jesus did without splitting under the weight of this world? As I pondered this, it occurred to me that maybe the simple answer is to take Jesus at his word. Maybe we lean in and listen to his clear directive to Peter in John 21:17: "Feed my sheep." Maybe this is the start of a revolution the world so severely needs.

If we want to be a people who feed Jesus' sheep, we need to be people who are deeply moved with great compassion for the people walking this earth. We can't have change without first having our hearts awakened to the situations our fellow image bearers are in. Are we stirred by the current state of affairs? Are we trusting that God placed us here for just such a time as this? Are we awake? Are our eyes open?

If you are shying away from bringing the hardships of the world to your table, can I be the first to say I am the most cowardly of us all? For a long time, I sat back with the pain of the world and tried to close my curtains tighter and tighter. More light-blocking curtains, please! I found myself thinking, *You don't need to worry about that thing that happened in another state*, or, *You can just turn off the news now, because that is not your issue, honey.* Or the one I always shamefully hope is true: *Whoa! You are not like that* at all. *You aren't prejudiced at all. You don't hate at all. Nope. Thank goodness you can wipe your hands of that mess.*

But the kind of hatred running around in the world today should make us turn inward. We need to look at ourselves. If we're pointing fingers, we need to point at ourselves. We don't need to find a stage, a podium, or a platform to start a revolution to heal the world. We just need to find our way to the table.

Listen, if we want to make the world a better place, if we want to be the light, we need to take the issues of the world and bring them into our homes. We need to sit and think deeply about subjects like race—*How in my life do I display racism? How in my life do I show anything less than love toward people who do not look like me or think like me or talk like me?* If we can sit down and do the hard work of asking the Holy Spirit to reveal our own ugliness and prejudices and then take the next step of countering those biases through the intentional relationships we foster at our tables, we can become lights in the darkness. We can show people what it's like to love in the midst of hatred and fear. This is a hard and holy work, which is why starting at the table should be our first step. It's a safe place. It's the place where Jesus started, and it's a place where he wants to meet us.

This description from Simon Carey Holt, a theologian and professional chef, brings home the point:

> It is through the daily practice of the table that we live a life worth living. Through the table we know who we are, where we come from, what we value and believe. At the table we learn what it means to be family and how to live in responsible, loving relationships. Through the table we live our neighborliness

and citizenship, express our allegiance to particular places and communities, and claim our sense of home and belonging. At the table we celebrate beauty and express solidarity with those who are broken and hungry.[1]

And we all said, "Amen!" Solidarity at the table. The table breaks down the walls of social class and backgrounds and race. We are all one at the table, human beings receiving the necessary act of eating a meal. We are all citizens with one another. No other act of coming together so powerfully proclaims this.

Jesus often received severe blowback for eating with those who were known as notorious sinners of his day. The fact that Jesus had a conversation with these sinners would have been shock factor enough, but he took it a step further when he ate with them. Sharing a meal at a table with people the world may not naturally put us together with is a catalyst for transformation, because we do exactly what Jesus did. We express our humanness through the act of eating and proclaim, "We are the same." This is the beginning of revolution. Jesus rebuked those who wanted only the rich at their tables, the seemingly clean, the "I have it all together" tribe. If we want to invite Jesus to our tables, if we want to open the door for others at our tables to meet Jesus, then perhaps we invite the poor. The outcast. The marginalized. Perhaps we let Jesus' words haunt us:

"For I was hungry and you gave me no food, I was thirsty and you gave me no drink, I was a stranger and you did not welcome me, naked and you did not clothe me, sick and in prison and you did not visit me." Then they also will answer, saying, "Lord, when did we see you hungry or thirsty or a stranger or naked or sick or in prison, and did not minister to you?" Then he will answer them, saying, "Truly, I say to you, as you did not do it to one of the least of these, you did not do it to me." (Matthew 25:42–45)

The table in our homes is still one of the most vibrant places we can follow in the footsteps of Jesus and love others. Our tables should be places where we are deployed as his missionaries. They are more than a structure to carry a meal. Life can be born at the table when we simply serve our guests a meal, encourage them after a long day, and receive them the way Jesus received Mary Magdalene—tenderly, acceptingly, joyfully. The table can be a vibrant life source, creating disciples with the strongest of devotions to Jesus and revealing a love to people who have never met Jesus. If we will commit to show up, Jesus will show up. He is so faithful.

A few years ago, I found myself in a mud hut in Ecuador with my friend and fellow blogger Shannan Martin. I was leading another trip to share Compassion International's work with a group of bloggers. We crowded into the small room and painstakingly started plucking corn from the cobs. We were awful at this task. Kernels were leaping from our hands and falling everywhere but inside the bowl. But we sat and worked on this together as we listened to the mother of the house talk. Hers was a family living in desperate poverty. She shared about her eleven children and the struggles she faced raising them. She told us how she could barely feed her family even one meal a day, and when she could, it was always a watery corn soup. And beyond worries of simply getting enough to eat, there were the ever-looming problems that plagued the area: teen suicide, money and drug laundering, and human trafficking.

As we fumbled with our corncobs, our translator stopped the conversation. Leaning into Shannan and me, she pleaded, "This family, they are very hungry; I can tell. Do you have any snacks you can give them?"

Shannan and I responded in wide-eyed disbelief as we combed through our purses. We didn't even have a stick of gum between us. We sat helpless in that moment, though we knew we had the most delicious of snacks waiting for us back at our hotel room. For thirty more minutes we sat there, longing to help in ways that we were unable to. We finished our time with the family and, after giving them a gift of necessary household items, rice, and oil for cooking, we departed. Then we gathered around a table.

Shannan, Ruth, Ashley, and I got to work right there. We leaned into the places God had taken us. Though we were tired and empty of understanding, we knew we could not claim ignorance. We linked arms with one another and pushed hard into a suffering world. We knew it was uncomfortable, but we trusted it would not break us. Our broken Savior had conquered, and we chose not to just believe it with our words or songs but with our hearts. We claimed our citizenship of heaven right there in the act of discussing what it was we were called to do now that we had been exposed to the suffering of the world. We wrestled with reconciling the very real truth that we were born into privilege and had more than we could ever need, while most of the world barely shared one-tenth of our comforts.

Some of our conversations and thoughts seemed leaky with too many doubts and too much pain. But we knew Jesus was right there with us as we worked out our salvation with fear and trembling. At that table, we filled up on rice and beans and questions. *What can we do? Where is the hope? How do we become hope?* We cried and laughed and prayed. We took our lives and let God hard-wire them to the lives we had met on that trip. This work at the table made us more awake, more generous, and increasingly softer. Also? It made us feel less alone. We grew quieter, and that night we went to our computers and wrote about the hurting people we had met, pleading with our families and friends to enter the suffering world with us to help.

One week later I stepped off a red-eye flight and went straight into church for a volunteer appreciation dinner. This was the making of a disaster, as I was still so exposed with hurt. Raw to the touch. I thought that maybe the wisest place I could take myself was directly to bed, but my heart had another idea. So Jeremy and I entered the house of peace as we stepped into church and partook in a time of worship.

Of course, just a few minutes in I had to bury my head in Jeremy's chest so my loud sobs would be muffled. I let my soul breathe through grieving. The church surrounded me and prayed, and we talked about Ecuador. After the service Jeremy asked me what I needed. I thought about my bed again but then erupted with, "A meal." We went to a local restaurant, found a table, and went to work again. I brought the hurt of Ecuador to that space at 9:00 p.m. I showed Jeremy pictures of the family I had met and shared their stories. Then I looked up at Jeremy like a deer in headlights. As if to say, "What am I supposed to do with all this pain? With all this hurt?" He pulled me in close, and through prayer we interceded for a hurting people. Bringing the hurting world to our tables might feel small, or it might even seem elusive. But God is exposing each of us to a need right now. He wants to use us right now. It might be a local or a global need. If we can just start with bringing it to the table—where ideas can be shared, doubts worked out, faith shored up, and prayers whispered. If we can do this, then we can all lock arms with one another and claim our citizenship of another world. We can claim our oneness with one another.

There is a new-to-us book Jeremy and I are now reading at our table. It's called *Surprise the World* by Michael Frost. The subtitle actually had me hiding the book after Jeremy brought it home and recommended it as our new book for the table. The subtitle is *The Five Habits of Highly Missional People*. I rolled my eyes like, "Do I have to stand on a street corner and scream at people about Jesus?!" Nope. No, thank you. It's clear that I have a negative reaction to the word *missional*. Jeremy, of course, found where I hid the book a few weeks later. After we finished our meal one night, we sat out on our patio and he brought it out.

"How about you read just the introduction, and I will give you a foot rub?"

"What?! I cannot be bought!" I spouted, as I found myself thrusting my feet into his lap. I proceeded to drily read the book. Needless to say, it's now my new favorite book. I highly recommend it. It's especially perfect for the table.

Michael Frost told one story in the book that I have not been able to stop thinking about. It shocked me, then saddened me. It was about the early Christians and the revolutionary way they loved. Apparently, these Christians were loving so well that they caught the eyes of the fourth-century emperor, Julian. This emperor was afraid they were going to take over the empire. In fact, he was so scared about their love movement that he wrote a directive to his officials, in effect declaring that his officials must start out-loving the Christians. In Frost's words, Julian "decreed a system of food distribution be started and that hostels be built for poor travelers."[2] The emperor even went on to write:

> **TIP:** Try reading a book at your table that your family all agrees to read together. Commit to reading the first few pages of the chapter (rotate each night who reads) and then discuss the themes that emerge for the remainder of mealtime.

Why do we not observe that it is their benevolence to strangers, their care for the graves of the dead and the pretended holiness of their lives that have done the most to increase atheism [the Emperor called Christians atheists for their disbelief in gods]? . . . For it is disgraceful when . . . the imperious Galileans support not only their own poor but ours as well, all men see that our people lack aid from us.[3]

Later on, Julian became even more confused and outraged by all the Galileans' "love feasts." He noted that they were meeting to eat together sometimes twice a day, and he could not keep straight why they were gathering so frequently to share a meal.[4]

Can you imagine the president of the United States or the local government authorities meeting together today and saying, "Have you seen the Christians? They are doing so much. They are caring for the poor, they are loving their neighbors, they are going to the widows and the prisoners. They are doing so excellently that we do not have to do our jobs. And, for some reason, they eat together all the time, and when they do, they invite all sorts of people from all sorts of backgrounds that normally wouldn't associate with one another." Can you imagine the body of Christ, the church, being looked at as revolutionary? As so extravagantly loving and willing to care for and help and feed all those who cross our path?

We don't have that rap sheet now, do we? Most nonbelievers think church is something you attend on Sunday for a sermon and some music. Many nonbelievers think Christians are here to judge and condemn, not love or feed. But we can start small. We can do exactly what Jesus did when he entered this world to change all of humanity, to rescue the lost. He started and ended at the table. Jesus asked us to love our neighbor. We can start there. We can take those few steps to our neighbors' doors and knock. We can say, "Come and eat."

## PRAYER FOR THE TABLE

*Father, thank you for putting us exactly where you have us. The cities you have us in, the jobs you have us in, the neighborhoods you have us in. Help us every day to show up and to love a little more than we did yesterday. We trust you to provide, to give us wisdom, to show us our next step. May we start a revolution of love right at our tables.*

## QUESTIONS FOR THE TABLE

1. Discuss how God carried out his mission on this earth, that he came eating and drinking. Do you think there is still power in this today?
2. Were you as shocked by the emperor's assessment of the early Christians as I was? What stood out to you?
3. Do you believe God can use your coming to the table consistently to teach you how to love better, and that this can ultimately affect your neighborhood and community?

## RECIPE FOR THE TABLE

## STUFFED BELL PEPPERS

Serves 4 to 5.

*This is a savory and hearty recipe that will fill everyone up! It's the perfect meal to bring sustenance to the body as we link arms around a meal and allow God to use us for his glory.*

## Ingredients:

1 tablespoon coconut or olive oil
1 (8-ounce) package baby bella mushrooms, sliced
 (optional)
1/2 medium red onion, chopped
1 small zucchini, chopped (optional)
1 carrot, chopped (optional)
1 pound ground beef, 80 percent lean
2 garlic cloves, minced
1 1/2 cups marinara sauce (half of a 24-ounce jar)
1 handful of spinach, chopped
1 teaspoon salt
1/4 teaspoon pepper
1/4 teaspoon crushed red pepper (optional)
4 bell peppers, tops removed, then cored and seeded
Parmesan cheese (optional)

## Instructions:

Preheat the oven to 375 degrees.

 Heat the coconut oil in a medium-size pan over medium-high heat. Add the mushrooms and allow them to cook, without flipping them, for 5 to 8 minutes. Flip the mushrooms and cook (without touching) for another 5 minutes.

 Add the onion, zucchini, and carrot. Cook and stir until the onions are translucent, 3 to 5 minutes. Add the beef and the garlic. Break the beef apart with a spatula and cook for 8 minutes, until it's no longer pink.

 Add the marinara sauce, and stir to combine. Cover the pan, reduce the heat to low, and cook for 10 minutes. Add the spinach, salt, pepper, and crushed red pepper (if you like it spicy). Stir, cover, and cook for 5 minutes. Taste the mixture, and add more salt or pepper if needed.

Place the bell peppers in an 8-inch square baking dish. Spoon the meat mixture into the bell peppers.

Bake the peppers for 15 to 20 minutes. If you would like to top with cheese, sprinkle it on top after 15 minutes, then bake for an additional 5 minutes.

To see pictures of this meal, visit http://oursavorylife.com/paleo-stuffed-bell-peppers/.

## TRICK

Never underestimate a good jar of marinara sauce. I keep at least three jars on hand at all times for quick meal prep or days when I forgot to meal plan.

# Appendix A

## YOUR KITCHEN: AN ART DEN

Initially, my desire to eat food was the motivation behind my first steps into the kitchen every evening, but along the way I started wondering if I could flip my attitude and make it a little more enjoyable? What if, instead of looking at it as entering the dreaded kitchen—the one that is always messy, the one that holds memories of a few choice words and a lot of stress—what if I looked at it as though I were entering an art den? My art den. After all, when we cook, we are creating. I don't care if you take two pieces of white bread and place peanut butter in the middle (which, by the way, delicious!), you are creating something.

Embracing the kitchen and its vibrant land can become life-giving instead of depleting. When I began looking at my kitchen with this new perspective, I started to deeply appreciate the simple fact that God created us to eat and gave us the ability to cook our own food. Just look at all the things he gave us to create with: mangos and avocados and cilantro and fresh thyme and garlic. He gave us garlic. Amen! So, I decided to start calling my kitchen my art den.

Have you been into an artist's den or office or loft before? Remnants of the artist's work are everywhere. Paint brushes, paint, journals, books, clay, sheet music, and also simple inspirational things. I decided that if I wanted to be inspired to cook, if I wanted to enter my kitchen with excitement or joy, I needed to transform it. So I found some great printouts about cooking and eating, and I framed them and hung them in my kitchen. I bought a smock that I adore—by smock, of course, I mean apron. I purchased a few quality pots and pans and knives. And I put a speaker right on the counter where I chop, because cooking is nothing without your favorite jams playing at full blast. My den is not only the place I create meals; it is the place dance parties happen.

Artists will tell you they need good tools to work with. They have a favorite paintbrush or pen or a great hammer or preferred brand of instrument. Likewise, there are a few kitchen tools that make creating in the kitchen a much more pleasurable experience. The first is a good knife. If you have ever watched the Food Network on television, you have heard people talking about a good-quality knife. Another game-changing item is a good set of pots and pans. This includes a saucepan, a soup pot, a slow cooker, and a Dutch oven. I promise you these tools will change your time in the kitchen. I did not get these all at once. I took the money from the diamond earrings Jeremy thought I would want (turns out I'm not much of a diamond girl!) and invested in a few pots and pans to start my collection, and then I started saving for other necessary items. We eventually bought a KitchenAid mixer. We'd been gifted one for our wedding, but I had returned it immediately because I never thought I would need it! I also started to do research on kitchen staples needed around the holiday season. This helped immensely in terms of cost (both receiving things as gifts and taking advantage of big sales!). Today, whenever I step into my kitchen, I truly feel like an artist with everything I need set up around me and ready to create!

Find what you think will make time in the kitchen more pleasant. Something to play music? A favorite apron? A new floor mat? A few inspirational quotes to hang on your wall, like "Your work in here is keeping people alive!"? Whatever it is, invest a little bit into creating your art den. Changing my surroundings drastically changed my attitude. And if you're worrying about the size of your kitchen, know that you can make the same delicious meal in a tiny apartment kitchen that you can in a grand chef's kitchen. I know this from experience. It's all in your perspective! So shake off any worries you have. Go forth and create your art den.

# Appendix B

## RESOURCES FOR THE TABLE

Keeping books or games on or near the table can be a great visual reminder that coming together around a meal will be fulfilling. It is also a great way to initiate interesting conversation. Below are some books and games Jeremy and I have enjoyed. I also include some other resources for no-stress meals at the table.

1. **Our Q&A: 3-Year Journal for 2 People** by Potter Style (also available for individuals, kids, moms, and families). This is a fun way to track answers to questions through the years, and it helps kickstart conversation.

2. **Table Topics.** These cards work as conversation starters. It's fun to have a stack on your dinner table. Seventeen different packets cover topics ranging from sports to family to book clubs.

3. **The Antelope in the Living Room** by Melanie Shankle. This is a great book for couples! Jeremy and I laughed, agreed in shock, and reminisced all the way through Melanie's stories. It was so fun!

4. **Surprise the World: The Five Habits of Highly Missional People** by Michael Frost. This book is based on the BELLS model: *B*less others, *E*at together, *L*isten to the Spirit, *L*earn Christ, and understand yourself as *S*ent by God into others' lives. It was fascinating and challenging. The questions at the end of each chapter make great dinnertime conversation starters.

5. **Rory's Story Cubes.** Each cube, the size of a die, has illustrations on it, and as you roll the cubes you use the illustrations as prompts to tell a story. There are a variety of ways to use these cubes, and they always bring about a lot of creativity and laughter.

6. **Dinnertime candles.** We have a little pod of tea light candles on our table. They're simple, but I love to light them at every meal to create ambiance and make the table comforting and inviting.

7. **Butcher paper.** This is a cheap and great tablecloth! It also helps with cleanup. Just buy a roll and drape the paper over the table. Add crayons, and have fun doodling with your guests!

8. **An empty basket.** I have an empty wicker basket that I use specifically for clearing our dining room table for meals. Our table usually fills up throughout the day with mail, books, and journals. Instead of feeling overwhelmed that there is no space at the table when it comes time for dinner, I just throw everything in the basket. This allows us to use the table at a moment's notice without getting overwhelmed by the mess.

9. **A textbook.** Find something you and your family all want to learn about, and find a textbook on the subject. It's fun to learn together about something new, and it is a great way to engage our minds at the end of a long day.

10. **Memory Bible verse cards.** Pick a few verses that your family wants to commit to memory, and write them out on note cards to read and work on memorizing together when you're at the table. Learning a verse every few weeks together with Jeremy has been so fulfilling. It is also the only time in my life I have consistently been able to memorize Bible verses.

# Appendix C

## 21-DAY ADVENTURE AT THE TABLE

For a long time, Jeremy and I saw the value of coming to the table consistently, but what we needed to do it well was a radical change. We needed a shift in our routines and attitudes. We knew the best way to create a habit is to dive into a routine, so we committed to intentionally coming to the table for twenty-one days. We completed the exercise over the course of one month and saw that it not only created a shift in habits but also a priceless growth in our relationship.

### WHY TWENTY-ONE DAYS?

There are some things in life that are not going to allow us to come to the table every single night. Kids with extracurricular activities or travel for work may keep us away from home at dinnertime. We wanted to create a system that allowed a lot of grace, so we would not get discouraged. During a thirty-day month, we included nine grace days. As you're gearing up for this challenge, know that however long you need to finish the twenty-one–day challenge is fine. Even if it takes you two months, that is a start! The goal is to increase the number of times you gather around the table. You know your family and your season of life better than anyone else, so factor that in and create something that will not stress you out or cause you great discouragement.

## HOW TO START

Because this was completely foreign to Jeremy and me when we first started, we sat down and created a few guidelines to help us succeed:

- Every Sunday evening we pulled out our calendars and marked the evenings during that week we could gather for meals at the table. This both set expectations and gave us flexibility.
- We also planned out meals for the week on Sunday. This helped ease the stress of "What are we eating tonight?"
- We selected a book we wanted to go through (or questions, cards, or something to learn). This helped us get excited about what our time at the table could look like.

Feel free to make use of what worked for us or come up with a whole new set of practices that work better for you. To help guide you on this adventure, I am including twenty-one meals for dinner, as well as a prayer and questions for the table. Each meal feeds four to five people (depending on how much your people eat!), and the recipes can easily be doubled. All recipes use real ingredients and are predominantly grain-free or paleo. They are also all 100 per-cent delicious and neighbor approved!

The first twelve days mirror the twelve chapters of this book, so you can go through the book as a family. Then the remaining nine days of the adventure allow us to continue the journey beyond what we've talked about already, which I hope will help you get a rhythm for how to start making your own versions of each day's plan to keep going into the future! But if you're ready now to do the challenge with your own ideas, feel free to get creative and cook your own meals or bring your own questions/activities/prayers to the table.

## DAY 1

### PRAYER FOR THE TABLE

*Jesus, thank you. Thank you for meeting us exactly where we are. In our own homes, at our own tables. Thank you for meeting our basic need so that we can have a window into our deepest need: your saving grace. May we receive not just this food we are about to eat but also your great love. The love that provides. The love that prepares a place for us at the table. Amen.*

### QUESTIONS FOR THE TABLE

1. Take time to reflect on all the different tables God has placed you at over the years. Share a favorite memory from a meal you have had in your life.
2. What was so amazing about that meal? Was it the food? Or the people? Was it the conversation? Or just the way you felt?
3. What are your thoughts on how many times Jesus appeared at a meal in the Gospels? Is this new to you? Why do you think it is significant?
4. Is there anyone in your life right now who, like Elijah, might be at

the end of his or her rope? Plan as a family to bring that person a meal or to invite him or her over to share a meal with you.

RECIPE FOR THE TABLE

## THE EASIEST AND TASTIEST ROAST

**Serves 5 to 6.**

*Think of this recipe as a kickoff to your journey of coming to the table consistently and enjoying a meal with the people you love. It's the easiest recipe I have in my arsenal, and my friends have told me time and time again that it's one of the tastiest roasts they've had. The simplicity of this recipe is a great reminder to me that the focus at the table is not the meal. It's the people.*

## Ingredients:

1 (3-pound) chuck roast
1/2 teaspoon salt
1/4 teaspoon pepper
1 tablespoon olive oil
1 (16-ounce) jar pepperoncinis
5 whole garlic cloves, peeled

## Instructions:

Pat the roast dry. Season with salt and pepper on all sides.

Optional: Brown the roast before adding it to your slow cooker. Heat a large skillet over medium-high heat. Add the olive oil. When the oil is shimmering, add the roast, and brown it on each side for 1 to 2 minutes.

Add the roast to a slow cooker. Pour the whole jar of pepperoncinis, including the juice, over the roast. Add the garlic cloves. Cover and cook on low for 8 hours or on high for 4 hours. The meat is done when it easily shreds with a fork.

### Alternate cooking method: Dutch Oven

I like to cook this roast in my Dutch oven when I can. I do this so I can brown the roast before adding all the ingredients (which gives it great flavor), and because I love using my Dutch oven!

Preheat the oven to 325 degrees.

Season the roast on all sides with salt and pepper.

Heat a Dutch oven over medium-high heat. Add the olive oil. When the oil is shimmering, add the roast, and brown it on each side (1 to 2 minutes per side).

Remove the Dutch oven from the heat. Add the whole jar of pepperoncinis, with the juice, and the garlic cloves. Cover with the lid, and bake for 3 hours.

To see images of this meal, visit http://oursavorylife.com/the-easiest-paleo-roast-recipe/.

## DAY 2

### PRAYER FOR THE TABLE

*Lord, thank you for enjoying us. Thank you for loving us and desiring so strongly to walk with us every day. Thank you for sharing so many meals with us when you were here on this earth. Give us the grace to routinely set a place for ourselves at the table. Give us the joy to come to the table every evening with the family you placed in our homes. Change our hearts to be bearers of peace, love, and patience, not just bearers of a meal when we come to the table.*

## QUESTIONS FOR THE TABLE

1. Have you ever struggled with showing up at the table?
2. What are some of the obstacles keeping you from coming to the table every evening?
3. What are some creative or new ways that you can overcome these obstacles to start coming to the table with your family?
4. Have you entered a home and been treated the way Jesus was treated by Mary? (To read the full story, check out Luke 10:38–42.)
5. How can you treat others the way Mary treated Jesus?

## RECIPE FOR THE TABLE

## CHEESY FONTINA DIP

**Serves 5 to 6.**

*This dish is easy and creative. It is ooey-gooey cheese baked in the oven and then served with loads of fruits and vegetables. When you're short on time and looking to simplify so you can be more intentional about bringing hope, love, peace—and your actual self— to the table, try this quick, fun dish that has the added perk of being interactive!*

## Ingredients:
1 1/2 pounds Fontina cheese, cut into 1-inch cubes
1/4 cup olive oil
3 garlic cloves, thinly sliced
1 tablespoon minced fresh thyme leaves
1 teaspoon minced fresh rosemary
1 teaspoon kosher salt
1 teaspoon freshly ground black pepper

Carrots, green apples, cauliflower, broccoli, or other veggies for
dipping

## Instructions:

Preheat the broiler, and position the oven rack 5 inches from the
heat.

Add the cubes of Fontina to a cast-iron pan. Drizzle the olive
oil over the cheese.

Combine the garlic, thyme, rosemary, salt, and pepper, and
sprinkle the mixture over the cheese and olive oil.

Place the pan under the broiler for 6 minutes, until the cheese
is melted and bubbling and starts to brown.

Serve the cheese family-style right out of the oven in the
cast-iron pan (make sure to place a hot pad over the handle so no
one gets burned!). Place the fruit and veggies on a tray that is easily
accessible to your guests.

NOTE: You will want to eat this right out of the oven, so the cheese
does not harden. I usually wait until all the guests have arrived and
then pop it in the oven. If the cheese does harden, just place it back
under the broiler until it's melty again.

## DAY 3

### PRAYER FOR THE TABLE

*Jesus, thank you for modeling to us how we can love others well as you walked
this earth and consistently showed up to a meal with others. Thank you for
this daily ritual of eating that can be used by you to create community right
where you have us. Grant us vision and bravery as we step out into our
neighborhoods, our work places, our communities and invite others over to a*

*meal. May we be controlled by your Spirit as we step out. May we extend the invitation and trust you to do the rest.*

## QUESTIONS FOR THE TABLE

1. Share a story or a memory you have about being invited to a table, especially during a time when you really needed the invitation. If you do not have one, ask God to bring someone onto your path to show you the power of being invited to come and eat.
2. Is there anything that is holding you back from inviting people to your table? What is it, and how can you overcome it?
3. "Come and eat!" is such a simple invitation, and it is the invitation Jesus used often. Are you drawn to the simplicity of this invitation? Are there ways you complicate the invitation for your friends or family to come to the table?

## RECIPE FOR THE TABLE

## EASY, DELICIOUS BOLOGNESE SAUCE WITH SWEET POTATO NOODLES

Serves 4 to 5.

*I learned a long time ago that I'm more likely to invite people to my table if I have some easy and delicious recipes in my arsenal that I know turn out well every time. This recipe is one from my mom, and if I could, I would eat it every night. I have also been known to eat spoonfuls of this sauce before even serving it over noodles. It's that good! Make plenty of this recipe to serve all your guests, and if you have leftovers, this tastes amazing the next day!*

## Ingredients:
2 tablespoons olive oil

1/2 red onion, diced

1 pound ground beef, 80 percent lean

3 garlic cloves, minced

1 tablespoon dried oregano

1/4 teaspoon crushed red pepper (optional)

1 1/4 cups dry red wine (or beef stock), divided

1 (28-ounce) can crushed tomatoes

2 tablespoons tomato paste

1 tablespoon salt

1/2 teaspoon pepper

1/4 cup heavy cream

1/2 cup freshly grated Parmesan cheese

1 sweet potato, peeled and spiralized (for sweet potato noodles) or 1
    (16-ounce) package spaghetti

## Instructions:

Heat the olive oil in a large skillet over medium-high heat. Add the onion, and cook until softened, about 3 minutes.

Add the ground beef, and cook, crumbling the meat with a spatula, for 5 to 7 minutes, until it begins to brown.

Stir in the garlic, oregano, and crushed red pepper, and cook for 1 more minute.

Pour 1 cup of the wine (or beef stock) into the skillet, stirring to scrape up any browned bits.

Add the tomatoes, tomato paste, salt, and pepper, and stir until combined. Bring to a boil, reduce the heat to low, and simmer for 10 minutes, uncovered.

Add the cream and the remaining 1/4 cup wine (or beef stock) to the sauce. Simmer for 8 to 10 minutes, stirring occasionally until thickened. Turn off the heat, and stir in the Parmesan cheese.

Bring a large pot of water to a boil. Add the spiralized sweet potato noodles. Boil for 4 to 6 minutes but no longer than 6 minutes. Drain the noodles. (If using spaghetti noodles, cook them according to the package directions.)

Place the noodles on a plate, and spoon the sauce on top. Sprinkle with more Parmesan cheese if desired.

To see photos of this recipe and how to spiralize the sweet potato, visit http://oursavorylife.com/how-to-make-sweet-potato-noodles/.

## DAY 4

### PRAYER FOR THE TABLE

*Father, thank you for choosing us to pour out your love into the world. Thank you for giving us a common way to show and practice and accept your love: inviting others to come and eat. Grant us a vision for what you want to see happen around our table. Illuminate the specific gifts you have given me and the needs you want to meet at my table, so I and the people under this roof can partner with you to fulfill your will.*

### QUESTIONS FOR THE TABLE

1. Do you have a life verse or current mission statement?
2. What specific kinds of people are most often at your table or what specific needs do you see consistently met at your table?
3. Grab a piece of paper, write out your verse, and fill out two columns of actions and outcomes you want to see happen at your table. What themes do you see presented in the columns and verse?
4. As a family, write out a vision. Remember that you can start out with a longer statement and then simplify.

**BONUS:** Once you've written your vision, go to your table the next night with some pens or crayons or paint and write your vision on a large piece of paper. Then hang it in a place where you all can see it! Also, there is no timestamp. It took weeks for Jeremy and me to land on a vision that was simple, one we could memorize, and also one that embodied our desire for our table.

## RECIPE FOR THE TABLE

## BALSAMIC GLAZED PORK

**Serves 5 to 6.**

*This recipe is a quick, no-fuss meal with lots of options for serving, so you can focus less on the food and enjoy more time with your people as you gather to discover a vision for your table!*

## Ingredients:
1 (2- to 3-pound) boneless pork tenderloin, fat trimmed
1/4 teaspoon salt
1/4 teaspoon pepper
1 cup chicken or vegetable broth
1/2 cup balsamic vinegar
2 tablespoons apple cider vinegar
1 tablespoon honey
3 garlic cloves, smashed
1 yellow onion, quartered
1 1/2 cups basmati rice
Oil for cooking eggs
5 to 6 eggs (or 1 egg per person)

## Instructions:
Rub the pork all over with salt and pepper.

In a small bowl mix together the broth, balsamic vinegar, apple cider vinegar, and honey.

Place the pork in a slow cooker, and pour the liquid all over the pork. Place the garlic and onion around the pork.

Cook on low for 6 to 8 hours or on high for 4 hours. The meat should easily shred with two forks.

When the pork is finished, let it rest, and cook the basmati rice according to the package instructions.

Place a large, nonstick skillet over medium heat. Add the oil, and when the oil is hot, crack a few eggs into the pan. (My pan holds three eggs at a time.) Allow the eggs to cook for about 1 minute. Reduce the heat to low, cover with a lid, and allow the eggs to cook for an additional 2 minutes. The eggs are done (over-easy) when a white film has formed over top of the eggs, but yolk is still liquidy.

To serve, remove the pork from the slow cooker and shred with two forks. Spoon some basmati rice onto a plate. Top with balsamic pork, and be sure to get some of the juices and onions onto the rice. Top with the over-easy egg.

ADDITIONAL SERVING OPTIONS: You can also serve the shredded pork on top of baked sweet potatoes (cooked in the oven at 400 degrees for 40 minutes). Or serve the pork on hamburger buns with sweet potato fries.

## DAY 5

### PRAYER FOR THE TABLE

*Jesus, you came not for the healthy but for the sick. You ate at the tables of tax collectors and sinners. May we be so willing to have the hurting at our table. May we not be made uncomfortable or distant by their hurt, but may we move ever closer to them by your power. If we are the hurting ones, give us the grace and patience to keep showing up at the table. May we all find you and usher you to our tables of brokenness.*

## QUESTIONS FOR THE TABLE

1. Have you eaten at a broken table? What was that like for you? Describe how you felt, what you thought, and where you saw Jesus in the brokenness. If you are in a season of eating at broken tables, take heart. Jesus ate at many broken tables. He knows exactly what you are facing, he sees you, and he is your anchor.
2. Do you have a story about a time when you received healing at a table? Why was there healing? Was it a kind question? Or a listening ear? Or a patient host?
3. How can you demonstrate the hope and love of Jesus at tables with the broken?

### RECIPE FOR THE TABLE

## CHICKEN CURRY WITH CAULIFLOWER RICE

Serves 4.

*Sometimes sitting at broken tables requires serving comfort food. Just as my Diet Coke became a sort of tangible anchor as I entered into long and complicated conversations in Thailand, comfort food can help anchor us. Takeout has always been my favorite comfort food—so much so that I learned how to make my own curry.*

## Ingredients:

## Curry:
1/4 cup (1/2 stick) unsalted butter
2 medium onions, finely chopped
2 large garlic cloves (or 3 small cloves), finely chopped
1 tablespoon peeled and finely minced fresh ginger
3 tablespoons curry powder

2 teaspoons salt

1 teaspoon ground cumin

1/2 teaspoon cayenne pepper (optional)

2 (8-ounce) boneless, skinless chicken breasts, cut into 1-inch
cubes

1 (14.5-ounce) can diced tomatoes

3/4 cup full-fat canned coconut cream

3/4 cup cashews, finely ground

## Cauliflower Rice:

1 head cauliflower

1/4 cup chicken stock

1 teaspoon garlic powder

1 1/2 teaspoons salt

1 cup golden raisins

1/4 cup roughly chopped cashews

## Instructions:

To prepare the curry, heat the butter in a large skillet over
medium-low heat until it is melted and slightly bubbling. Add the
onions, garlic, and ginger. Cook and stir until softened, about 5
minutes.

Add the curry powder, salt, cumin, and cayenne (omit the
cayenne if you do not like spicy curry), and cook, stirring to coat
the onion mixture with the spices, for 1 minute.

Add the chicken and cook, stirring to coat, for 3 minutes.

Add the tomatoes, including the juice, and bring the mixture
to a simmer. Cover and allow to simmer for 20 minutes, stirring
occasionally.

Uncover and add the coconut cream. Stir, cover, and simmer
for 20 minutes, stirring occasionally.

Add the finely ground cashews. Stir and cook for 5 minutes.

To prepare the cauliflower rice, wash and dry the cauliflower. Remove the greens, and cut the head into 4 sections.

To grate the cauliflower, use a box grater or a food processor with the grater attachment.

Add the grated cauliflower to a medium pot, along with the chicken stock, garlic powder, and salt. Turn the heat to medium, cover, and allow to steam for 7 minutes. Uncover and stir to fluff. Stir in the raisins and chopped cashews.

Serve the curry over the cauliflower rice.

NOTE: You can also use basmati rice in place of the cauliflower rice. Follow the instructions on the package, and add the raisins and cashews at the end. Serve the curry over the rice.

To see pictures of this recipe, visit http://oursavorylife.com/ chicken-curry-recipe-paleo-rice/.

## DAY 6

### PRAYER FOR THE TABLE

*Jesus, thank you for letting us participate in your great work. Thank you for calling us to extend ourselves and our food and to trust you with everything else. May we do the holy and honored work of practicing hospitality, so that we might be your hands and feet to a hurting world. Amen.*

### QUESTIONS FOR THE TABLE

1. Have you ever received gracious hospitality from the poor? Describe your encounter.
2. What are some unique ways God has gifted you to show hospitality?
3. What is one way you can love a stranger this month?

# IT'S DONE ALREADY? CHICKEN SALSA SOUP

**Serves 5 to 6.**

*This soup is a one-pot wonder, and it takes minutes from start to finish. It's perfect for last-minute guests and a great way to keep you out of the kitchen and, instead, at the table.*

## Ingredients:

1 tablespoon olive oil
1/2 medium white onion, diced
2 garlic cloves, diced
6 cups chicken stock or chicken broth
Juice of 2 limes
2 cups shredded rotisserie or precooked chicken
1 (15-ounce) can white cannellini beans, drained (optional)
1 cup frozen corn (optional)
1 (16-ounce) jar tomatillo salsa
Toppings for serving, such as hot sauce, sour cream, shredded
    Cheddar cheese, fresh cilantro, sliced avocado, and lime wedges

## Instructions:

Heat a large pot or Dutch oven over medium-high heat. Add the olive oil, and when the oil is hot, add the diced onion and garlic. Cook, stirring, for about 3 minutes, until the onion is softened.

Add the chicken broth, lime juice, shredded chicken, beans, corn, and salsa.

Allow the soup to simmer for 10 to 15 minutes, stirring occasionally. To serve, let your guests ladle out some soup, and have toppings set out for them to add to the soup.

# DAY 7

## PRAYER FOR THE TABLE

*Father, we come to you just as we are. We come home after a day at war with our flesh. We come home feeling like we may have lost a few battles, like we missed the mark of your calling. But we look to you for our peace tonight. We look to you, because we know you have not forsaken us. You have not called us back to our former life apart from you, but you draw us ever nearer, reminding us that we do, in fact, love you more than this world and what it has to offer. Fill us with your peace that reminds us you won the war. Fill us with your peace as we share a meal.*

## QUESTIONS FOR THE TABLE

1. Do you have a memory of receiving a meal that brought great peace? Was that peace the result of the company or the food itself, or both?

2. What do you most want people to leave your table feeling? Is it peace? Did you find peace at your table growing up? How can we usher the peace of God to our table? The peace that pardons us, that reminds us we are covered by his sacrifice, that is Jesus' voice to us, saying,

> Are you tired? Worn out? Burned out on religion? Come to me. Get away with me and you'll recover your life. I'll show you how to take a real rest. Walk with me and work with me—watch how I do it. Learn the unforced rhythms of grace. I won't lay anything heavy or ill-fitting on you. Keep company with me and you'll learn to live freely and lightly. (Matthew 11:28–30, THE MESSAGE)

## CILANTRO LIME FISH TACOS

**Serves 4 to 5.**

*In honor of the meal Jesus ate and prepared several times, let's make fish! Mahi mahi is a mild-tasting fish with a firm texture that makes it great for grilling. These tacos are filled with flavor thanks to the marinade. People who don't like fish have told me they love this meal.*

## Ingredients:

2 garlic cloves, peeled
1 cup cilantro leaves, loosely packed
Juice of 2 limes
2 teaspoons ground cumin
2 teaspoons kosher salt
1 teaspoon freshly ground black pepper
1 pound mahi mahi
Oil for the grill
Corn tortillas, warmed (2 small corn tortillas per person)
Toppings such as sour cream, extra cilantro, salsa, lime wedges,
    cheese, avocados

## Instructions:

Place the garlic, cilantro leaves, lime juice, cumin, salt, and black pepper in a food processor, and pulse until all ingredients are roughly chopped and combined. Be sure to scrape down the sides of the bowl to combine everything.

Place the mahi mahi in a 1-gallon resealable plastic bag, and add the herb mixture. Set the fish aside to marinate at room temperature for 15 to 20 minutes.

Heat the grill to medium-high heat, and liberally coat the

grates with oil. Remove the fish from the marinade (discard the marinade), and place the fish on the grill. Grill 4 minutes per side.

Place the fish in a bowl, and roughly shred it with two forks.

Add the fish to warmed tortillas (we like to throw our tortillas on the grill for a few seconds), and allow everyone to add their favorite toppings.

NOTE: You can also cook the fish on the stove by preheating a nonstick pan over medium-high heat. Add 1 tablespoon of oil, and when it begins to shimmer, add the fish. Cook for 4 to 5 minutes per side, until it easily flakes with a fork.

## DAY 8

### PRAYER FOR THE TABLE

*Jesus, thank you for your sacrifice. Thank you that you modeled a way for us to remember what you did for us. A way to remember that there is now no condemnation for us in you. Holy Spirit, grant us wisdom as we desire to participate in a communion that is holy and unrushed. May we be part of many little rehearsals before the grand marriage banquet.*

### QUESTIONS FOR THE TABLE

1. One unique way of bringing communion to your table is to take some time to share your testimony over a meal. If you've already shared it with your people, find a creative way to share it again. Try doing it in new and varied ways: in three sentences or less, only using verbs, or even in a riddle or a haiku. This is your personal great remembering of how Jesus saved you.
2. What is a favorite memory you have of taking communion? Why was it so special?

3. What are your thoughts about taking communion inside your home with your people? If you are interested, plan a time and date to perform this ritual for the first time.

RECIPE FOR THE TABLE

## THIN CRUST PIZZA

*This is the pizza recipe Jeremy and I made in the communion story I shared. It's quite fitting for communion because it's a grain-free dough—so it's unleavened. We have made this pizza for extreme pizza lovers, and though it is more of a thin-crust style, people of all crust preferences have loved it!*

## Ingredients:
1 cup tapioca flour
1/4 cup potato flour
1 teaspoon dried Italian herbs
1/4 teaspoon garlic powder
1/4 cup grated Parmesan cheese (optional)
1/3 cup water
1 teaspoon powdered unflavored gelatin
1 egg
1/4 cup extra-virgin olive oil
1 tablespoon harissa oil or 1/4 teaspoon crushed red pepper (optional)
1 tablespoon melted butter (optional)
Sprinkle of fleur de sel (optional)
Toppings such as pizza sauce, mozzarella cheese, pepperoni, bell peppers, red onions

## Instructions:
Preheat the oven to 400 degrees. Place a 13-inch pizza stone or large cast-iron skillet in the oven to preheat.

In a large bowl mix together the tapioca flour, potato flour, dried Italian herbs, garlic powder, and Parmesan cheese, if using.

In a small bowl add the water, and sprinkle the gelatin over the water. Add the egg and oils, and whisk to combine.

Add the egg mixture to the flour mixture and mix together (I use my hands for this part). A dough should start to form. If the dough is too dry, add water by the teaspoon. The dough should hold together but not be sticky. Keep the dough in the bowl until the pizza stone is ready.

Take the pizza stone out of the oven. Place the dough on the pizza stone, and roll it out to 1/4-inch thickness and about 10 inches in diameter. Be careful, as the stone will be hot! Remember that this is not regular pizza dough. The first few times we made this we did not get it into a perfect circle, but that is okay!

If desired, brush melted butter on the edges of the dough, and sprinkle with fleur de sel.

Bake the dough for 15 to 20 minutes, until it's golden brown around the edges.

Remove the pizza crust from the oven, and coat with pizza sauce and desired toppings. Put the pizza back in the oven for another 15 to 20 minutes until the cheese is melted. Remove from the oven, slice into wedges, and enjoy!

To see pictures of this recipe, visit http://oursavorylife.com/homemade-paleo-pizza-crust/.

## DAY 9

### PRAYER FOR THE TABLE

*Jesus, thank you for coming as you did—as a babe and then a humble servant. Never calling on your power or position but kneeling and sacrificing. May we lean into your life and make it our own. Stir us, Holy Spirit, as we come to the table at the end of the day, to pour ourselves out in service. Use us all up, and then fill us again.*

## QUESTIONS FOR THE TABLE

1. How have you seen meekness or humility practiced at the table over a meal?
2. Have you struggled with meekness? How so?
3. Is there someone in your life who embodies a "there you are" mentality? What about them communicates that they are more about others than themselves?
4. What is one thing you can change at your table to consistently practice humility?

## RECIPE FOR THE TABLE

## WHITE CHICKEN CHILI

Serves 5 to 6.

*This soup is packed with flavor and extremely simple to make, so no unnecessarily complicated instructions here. You can use leftover chicken or buy a rotisserie chicken and just pull the meat off the bones (you can freeze the leftover meat for up to one month). This recipe helps us get to the table quicker so we can focus more on serving the people at our table, not just serving a meal.*

## Ingredients:

1 tablespoon coconut oil
1 medium onion, chopped
2 cups shredded cooked chicken
1 1/2 teaspoons garlic powder
2 1/4 cups chicken broth, divided

1 (15.5-ounce) can Great Northern beans, rinsed and drained

1 cup frozen corn (optional)

4 ounces fresh roasted and chopped green chiles (or one 4-ounce can chopped green chiles)

1 teaspoon salt

1 teaspoon ground cumin

1 teaspoon dried oregano

1/2 teaspoon black pepper

1/4 teaspoon cayenne pepper

1 cup plain Greek yogurt (optional)

1/2 cup heavy whipping cream (optional)

## Instructions:

Heat a large pot or Dutch oven over medium heat. Add the coconut oil, and allow it to melt. Add the onion, and cook until translucent, stirring occasionally, about 3 minutes.

Add the shredded chicken and garlic powder, and stir to combine. Pour in 1/4 cup of the chicken broth and stir, scraping the bottom of the pot to loosen any browned bits. Cook for 2 minutes.

Add the remaining 2 cups chicken broth, beans, corn, chiles, salt, cumin, oregano, and black and cayenne peppers. Turn the heat to high, and bring to a boil. Then reduce the heat to medium-low and simmer, uncovered, for 30 minutes.

Taste the soup, and add additional salt or pepper if needed. The soup may be served like this, or for a super creamy chili, remove the pot from the heat, and stir in the Greek yogurt and cream. Serve warm.

To learn how to make batches of your own roasted green chiles (which will last in the freezer for up to three months), visit http://oursavorylife.com/substitute-for-canned-green-chilies/.

For step-by-step pictures of this recipe, visit http://oursavorylife.com/white-chicken-chili-recipe-2/.

## DAY 10

### PRAYER FOR THE TABLE

*Father, thank you for life! Thank you for allowing us to live, and thank you for all the curious and wonderful and even mundane things we get to bump into every day. Help us pay attention. Help us choose to show up to what you are doing in our lives. Give us your strength and your grace to live each day awake and then to come to our tables in the evening and share the stories of all the things you did through us.*

### QUESTIONS FOR THE TABLE

1. Is your table a place for stories? Are your people encouraged in the art of storytelling around the table? What makes your table either an inviting or uninviting place for stories?
2. Share one interesting story from your day. Make sure to tell it in story form. You are a storyteller. Transport the people around your table to the story you are sharing using imagery and sights and smells and even different inflections in your voice.
3. How can you encourage more stories around your table? Maybe on Thursday nights you can have a story slam around your table, where everyone gets five minutes to share a story and vote anonymously (maybe on pieces of paper placed in a hat) on their favorite story.

### RECIPE FOR THE TABLE

## A PALEO BREAKFAST RECIPE: SWEET POTATO HASH

Serves 4.

*In loving memory of my great-grandma Smith, the person I most loved eating breakfast with, whose stories at the table still echo bright, we're*

*going to have breakfast for dinner! This breakfast scramble is one of my*
*favorites. I especially love it because it's savory. You can serve it with*
*eggs and bacon and even the pancakes of your liking.*

## Ingredients:

5 strips bacon

2 large sweet potatoes, scrubbed and cubed (you can leave the skin
   on)

1 teaspoon salt

1/4 teaspoon pepper

1/2 teaspoon onion powder

1 tablespoon coconut oil

1 red or white onion, chopped

1/2 poblano pepper, chopped

2 garlic cloves, thinly sliced

1 tablespoon olive oil

2 to 4 eggs (depending on how many people you are serving)

## Instructions:

In a cast-iron skillet or frying pan over medium-high heat, cook
the bacon until crispy. Remove the bacon, and place it on a paper
towel–lined plate. Pour all but 1 tablespoon of the bacon fat out of
the skillet, and reduce the heat to medium.

Add the cubed sweet potatoes to the skillet. Add the salt,
pepper, and onion powder, and stir to coat the potatoes. Cover the
skillet, and cook for 5 minutes, without stirring, so the potatoes can
caramelize. Flip the potatoes, and cover again. Cook for 5 more
minutes without stirring. Flip the potatoes once more, and allow to
cook for 8 more minutes uncovered. Remove the potatoes and set
them aside.

Add the coconut oil to the skillet, increase the heat to
medium-high, and add the onions, poblano pepper, and garlic.

Cook and stir for about 3 minutes until softened. Add the sweet potatoes back to the skillet. Stir and allow the hash to cook for 2 more minutes.

Taste the sweet potatoes to make sure they are cooked through. They should be browned on the outside but pillowy in the center, firm but not crunchy. Add more salt and pepper if desired.

Place another skillet over medium-high heat, and add the olive oil. When the oil is heated, crack the eggs into the pan. Allow to cook until the whites are set but the yolks are still runny, 2 to 3 minutes. Serve the sweet potato hash with eggs and bacon.

NOTE: If you'd like to keep the dish vegetarian, skip the bacon, and add 1 tablespoon coconut oil to the skillet before you add the sweet potatoes.

For step-by-step pictures of this recipe, visit http://oursa-vorylife.com/paleo-breakfast-recipe-sweet-potato-hash/.

## DAY 11

### PRAYER FOR THE TABLE

*Father, thank you for trusting us to be salt in this earth. To carry your love and your peace to everyone on our path. May we be brave enough to ask and allow room for questions at our table, finding peace and knowing that we do not need all the answers. Trusting that you can use just a little bit of our love and compassion to reveal yourself to someone.*

### QUESTIONS FOR THE TABLE

1. What do you think it means to be salt of the earth? What does it look like to bring salt to your table?

2. Is there a question (or questions) you have been asking internally that you can share at the table? Take a moment to think about what God has been speaking to you. For example, maybe he has been teaching you more about grace, and perhaps you can ask, "Am I a grace-filled person?" or "How can I show more grace?"

3. As a family, have you come up with some safe rules at the table? For example, Jeremy and I are very clear with our expectations when we want to ask a hard question. I might say, "I have a question I need to ask out loud, but I am not looking for an answer. I am looking for you to listen and pray." This can help preempt him trying to answer me when I just need to talk.

4. How can you allow more room for questions at the table?

## RECIPE FOR THE TABLE

## THE BEST BURGER RECIPE

**Serves 6.**

*This is the burger recipe we made for Jeff. It's great for those moments when you invite a new person over and want a casual night where everyone's at ease and feels they can share their hearts. We served it on sweet potato buns. And, of course, added the bacon.*

## Ingredients:

2 tablespoons Worcestershire sauce
1 tablespoon extra-virgin olive oil
1 tablespoon garlic powder
1 1/2 teaspoons onion powder
1/2 teaspoon salt
1/4 teaspoon pepper
2 1/2 pounds ground chuck, 80 percent lean
2 tablespoons butter, cut into 6 cubes

## Instructions:

Preheat a grill or grill pan over medium heat.

In a medium bowl mix together the Worcestershire sauce, olive oil, garlic powder, onion powder, salt, and pepper. Add the ground chuck, and massage the spice mixture into the meat.

Form 6 tennis ball–sized balls with the meat. Create a patty by flattening the ball out with your palms.

Take a pinch of meat out of the center of each patty and place a cube of butter in the indentation (this will keep the burgers from drying out while they cook). Place the meat back on each patty, fully covering the butter.

Grill the patties for 6 minutes on the first side and 4 to 5 minutes on the second side for medium. Leave them on for an additional 2 minutes for well done.

Let the burgers rest for 5 minutes. Serve with your favorite condiments.

To see pictures of this recipe and the recipe for sweet potato buns, visit: http://oursavorylife.com/the-best-burger-recipe-so-good-the-bun-gets-in-the-way/.

## DAY 12

### PRAYER FOR THE TABLE

*Father, thank you for putting us exactly where you have us. The cities you have us in, the jobs you have us in, the neighborhoods you have us in. Help us every day to show up and to love a little more than we did yesterday. We trust you to provide, to give us wisdom, to show us our very next step. May we start a revolution of love right at our tables.*

## QUESTIONS FOR THE TABLE

1. Discuss how God carried out his mission on this earth, that he came eating and drinking. Do you think there is still power in this today?
2. Were you as shocked by the emperor's assessment of the early Christians as I was? What stood out to you? (Refer to chapter 12 for the full story.)
3. Do you believe God can use your coming to the table consistently to teach you how to love better, and that this can ultimately affect your neighborhood and community?

## RECIPE FOR THE TABLE

## STUFFED BELL PEPPERS

**Serves 4 to 5.**

*This is a savory and hearty recipe that will fill everyone up! It's the perfect meal to bring sustenance to the body as we link arms around a meal and allow God to use us for his glory.*

## Ingredients:

1 tablespoon coconut or olive oil
1 (8-ounce) package baby bella mushrooms, sliced
    (optional)
1/2 medium red onion, chopped
1 small zucchini, chopped (optional)
1 carrot, chopped (optional)
1 pound ground beef, 80 percent lean
2 garlic cloves, minced
1 1/2 cups marinara sauce (half of a 24-ounce jar)

1 handful of spinach, chopped
1 teaspoon salt
1/4 teaspoon pepper
1/4 teaspoon crushed red pepper (optional)
4 bell peppers, tops removed, then cored and seeded
Parmesan cheese (optional)

## Instructions:

Preheat the oven to 375 degrees.

Heat the coconut oil in a medium-size pan over medium-high heat. Add the mushrooms and allow them to cook, without flipping them, for 5 to 8 minutes. Flip the mushrooms and cook (without touching) for another 5 minutes.

Add the onion, zucchini, and carrot. Cook and stir until the onions are translucent, 3 to 5 minutes. Add the beef and the garlic. Break the beef apart with a spatula and cook for 8 minutes, until it's no longer pink.

Add the marinara sauce, and stir to combine. Cover the pan, reduce the heat to low, and cook for 10 minutes. Add the spinach, salt, pepper, and crushed red pepper (if you like it spicy). Stir, cover, and cook for 5 minutes. Taste the mixture, and add more salt or pepper if needed.

Place the bell peppers in an 8-inch square baking dish. Spoon the meat mixture into the bell peppers.

Bake the peppers for 15 to 20 minutes. If you would like to top with cheese, sprinkle it on top after 15 minutes, then bake for an additional 5 minutes.

To see pictures of this meal, visit: http://oursavorylife.com/paleo-stuffed-bell-peppers/.

## DAY 13

---

### PRAYER FOR THE TABLE

*Jesus, thank you for this day and for your life poured out for us. Thank you not only for your sacrifice but also for walking with us each day. Grant us peace and comfort as we close out this evening.*

### QUESTIONS FOR THE TABLE

1. What was one thing that happened today that seemed odd or out of place?
2. If you could label today with one word, what would it be?
3. How did you see God show up in your day?

### RECIPE FOR THE TABLE

## WEDGE SALAD WITH HOMEMADE HERB DRESSING

---

Serves 6.

*This salad is so fresh while still being very filling! The creamy, homemade ranch dressing is irresistible and lasts up to one month in the refrigerator in an airtight container. It also comes together very quickly to make for a super-fast meal.*

## Ingredients:

## Herb Dressing:
3 green onions, white and green parts, chopped
1/2 cup chopped fresh basil leaves
1 tablespoon chopped fresh dill
2 tablespoons freshly squeezed lemon juice

1 1/2 tablespoons Dijon mustard
1 tablespoon olive oil
2 garlic cloves, chopped
1/2 teaspoon kosher salt
1 teaspoon freshly ground black pepper
1/2 cup plain Greek yogurt
1/2 cup heavy whipping cream

## Salad:

Iceberg lettuce, cut into 4 to 6 wedges or salad greens for 6
Cherry tomatoes, halved
Fried bacon, chopped
Red onion, sliced
Sharp Cheddar cheese, shredded
Any additional salad toppings you love

## Instructions:

Place the green onions, basil, dill, lemon juice, Dijon mustard, olive oil, garlic, salt, and pepper in the bowl of a food processor fitted with the steel blade. Puree for 15 to 20 seconds or until finely chopped. Add the Greek yogurt and heavy whipping cream, and blend until smooth. Transfer the dressing to a container with a lid, and refrigerate for 1 hour for the flavors to develop.

Allow everyone to assemble toppings on their wedge of lettuce. Drizzle with the herb dressing.

## DAY 14

### PRAYER FOR THE TABLE

*Father, thank you for the gift of being able to gather with people we love around a meal. Thank you for providing this food and for creating this day. Even as the day is closing, may we continue to draw near to you and accept your love.*

## QUESTIONS FOR THE TABLE

1. If you could host any kind of dinner party what would it be? Would there be a theme? What food would be served? Who would attend?
2. If you could cook one meal with anyone, who would it be?
3. What is currently bringing you great hope?

## RECIPE FOR THE TABLE

# HONEY MUSTARD CHICKEN BAKE WITH ROASTED VEGGIES

Serves 4.

## Ingredients:
1/3 cup honey
1/3 cup Dijon mustard
1 teaspoon apple cider vinegar
4 chicken thighs or 2 (8-ounce) chicken breasts, cut in half
3 tablespoons olive or coconut oil
1 teaspoon salt
1/2 teaspoon pepper
2 garlic cloves, minced
1 bunch broccoli, cut into florets
3 carrots, peeled and cut in thirds
1 red onion, quartered

## Instructions:
Preheat the oven to 350 degrees. Line a rimmed baking sheet or a 12 x 9-inch baking dish with aluminum foil. Grease the aluminum foil with butter or oil.

In a bowl mix together the honey, Dijon mustard, and apple cider vinegar. Place the chicken in the bowl, and roll the chicken in the sauce. Place the chicken in the middle of the baking sheet, and pour the remainder of sauce on top.

Place the oil, salt, pepper, and garlic in a large bowl, and stir to combine. Add the veggies, and toss to coat. Distribute the veggies on the baking sheet around the chicken.

Bake for 30 minutes. For extra-crispy vegetables, toss halfway through cooking time.

## DAY 15

### PRAYER FOR THE TABLE

*Jesus, thank you for modeling the practice of gathering around a meal. May we bless you as we come together and give thanks for your work in our lives. Please come join us as we make room for you at our table.*

### QUESTIONS FOR THE TABLE

1. If there is one thing you could change about the time you spend at your table during a meal, what would it be?
2. What book (besides the Bible) has most significantly influenced your life?
3. As a family, share thoughts about a book you would like to read and discuss together at the table. Make a plan to do just that.

### RECIPE FOR THE TABLE

## BUTTERNUT SQUASH LASAGNA

Serves 5 to 6.

Ingredients:
1 tablespoon olive oil

1 red onion, diced

1 pound ground beef, 80 percent lean

3 garlic cloves, minced

1 teaspoon salt

1/4 teaspoon pepper

1 (24-ounce) jar marinara sauce

1 small butternut squash

1 pound fresh mozzarella, shredded, divided

## Instructions:

Preheat the oven to 400 degrees.

Heat a large skillet over medium-high heat, and add olive oil. When the oil is hot, add the onion and cook, stirring, for 2 minutes. Add the ground beef, and cook for 8 minutes, until it is no longer pink. Use a spatula to break up the meat.

Add the garlic, salt, and pepper, and cook, stirring, for an additional 2 minutes. Add the marinara sauce. Reduce the heat to low, and let the mixture simmer for 5 minutes.

Cut the bulbous end off the butternut squash. This is where all the seeds live. Cut off the top with the stem, and discard. Peel the squash. Set the squash on its side, and cut it into thin rounds.

In a 9-inch square baking dish, place some of the squash in a single layer. Add some of the ground beef mixture. Add a layer of mozzarella. Repeat the layers until all the ingredients, except for about 1 cup of the cheese, are used. The last ingredient on the top should be the sauce.

Bake for 35 minutes. Remove the lasagna from the oven, and add the reserved cheese on top. Return the lasagna to the oven, and allow the cheese to melt and get bubbly, 5 to 10 more minutes.

Let the lasagna stand for 15 minutes to slightly cool and set before serving.

# DAY 16

## PRAYER FOR THE TABLE

*Jesus, we are reminded that when you came to this earth you did not start ministries or nonprofits; you simply called out to people and ate with them. Help us to do the same. Show us how you can use us to show more of your love through meals at our table.*

## QUESTIONS FOR THE TABLE

1. What was your favorite childhood meal?
2. Did meals around the table play a significant role in your childhood?
3. How can you take an aspect of Jesus' life and model it consistently around your table?

## RECIPE FOR THE TABLE

## CHICKEN POT PIE SOUP

Serves 5 to 6.

### Ingredients:

4 tablespoons butter

1/2 yellow onion, diced

4 carrots, thinly sliced

4 ribs celery, thinly sliced

3 cups shredded cooked chicken or turkey (or 2 pounds chicken breasts, cooked and shredded)

2 tablespoons arrowroot (or 1 tablespoon cornstarch)

1/4 teaspoon dried Italian herbs

1 teaspoon salt

1/4 teaspoon pepper

1/2 teaspoon dried sage

2 1/2 cups low-sodium chicken broth

1/4 cup heavy whipping cream or half-and-half

1/2 cup frozen peas (optional)

## Instructions:

Melt the butter in a large soup pot over medium-high heat. Add the onion, carrots, and celery. Cook, stirring, until the onions start to turn translucent, about 5 minutes.

Stir in the chicken or turkey, and sprinkle the arrowroot or cornstarch on top. Stir until it coats the meat and vegetables. (The starch is a thickening agent and will create a nice stew consistency.) Cook for 1 minute, then add the Italian herbs, salt, pepper, and sage. Stir to coat the veggies and meat with the herbs.

Pour in the chicken broth. Reduce the heat to low, and let simmer for 20 minutes. When it starts to thicken, stir in the cream. Let the sauce bubble up and thicken for about 3 minutes. If it seems overly thick, splash in a little more broth. Mix in frozen peas if using, and let cook for additional 2 minutes.

Taste and adjust seasoning to your liking. Serve warm.

## DAY 17

### PRAYER FOR THE TABLE

*Father, thank you for creating us so uniquely and intricately. May we honor you with our minds and our gifts. Holy Spirit, teach us how to steward well the lives God gave each of us.*

## QUESTIONS FOR THE TABLE

1. If you could go back to university and get a degree in anything, what would it be?
2. Discuss, as a family, if there is something you would all like to learn together. Perhaps a new language or memorizing Bible verses, or about another culture. How can you implement this at your table?
3. What is one thing about Jesus you always wanted to learn?

## RECIPE FOR THE TABLE

# HEARTY BEEF CHILI

Serves 5 to 6.

## Ingredients:

4 to 5 strips bacon
1 red bell pepper, chopped
1 poblano pepper, chopped
1 red onion, chopped
3 garlic cloves, chopped
1 jalapeño, seeds removed and chopped (omit if you do not want a spicy chili)
1 1/2 pounds ground sirloin (or 80 percent lean ground beef)
2 tablespoons tomato paste
2 teaspoons salt
1 tablespoon chili powder
1 teaspoon ground cumin
1/4 teaspoon cayenne pepper
1/2 cup red wine, beef stock, or beer
1 (28-ounce) can crushed tomatoes
1 (15-ounce) can black beans, drained and rinsed (optional)

## Instructions:

In a soup pot fry the bacon. Remove the bacon, and keep about 1 teaspoon of bacon fat in the pot. Chop the bacon for topping the chili. Set aside. (This step is optional. If you do not use the bacon, add 1 tablespoon of oil to the soup pot.)

Add the chopped peppers, onion, and garlic to the pot, and cook, stirring, over medium-high heat until the veggies are tender, for 3 to 4 minutes.

Add the beef, and cook until browned, about 5 minutes. Use a spatula to break up the meat as it cooks.

Add the tomato paste, salt, chili powder, cumin, and cayenne, and cook, stirring, about 2 minutes. Add the wine, and cook, scraping up any browned bits on the bottom of the pot. Add the crushed tomatoes (with juice) and beans. Bring to a boil. Reduce the heat to medium-low, and simmer for 10 minutes. Taste and add salt if needed.

Serve with hot sauce, sour cream, Cheddar cheese, crumbled bacon, jalapeños, cilantro, or anything else you like.

## DAY 18

### PRAYER FOR THE TABLE

*Lord, some of us are weary from the journey you have us on. Some of us are filled and brimming over with joy. Wherever you have us, use us, either to accept comfort and healing or to be a well of peace and joy to someone on our path.*

### QUESTIONS FOR THE TABLE

1. What would you say is your default emotion in this season of life? (It might be joy or stress or sorrow.) Why?

2. Read out loud the account of God feeding Elijah in 1 Kings 19:1–9. Have you been provided a meal (or have you provided a meal) that brought great healing and strengthened you for the journey God has you on?

3. Is there someone your family can bless now with a meal? It might be picking up groceries for them, inviting them over, or sending over a prepared meal. Brainstorm as a family and come up with a plan.

## RECIPE FOR THE TABLE

## TURKEY BURGERS WITH SWEET POTATO FRIES

Serves 4 to 5.

Ingredients:

### Sweet Potato Fries:
1 large or 2 small sweet potatoes
1/2 teaspoon salt
1/2 teaspoon freshly ground black pepper
1 teaspoon garlic powder
2 tablespoons olive oil

### Burgers:
1 pound ground chicken or ground turkey
1/2 tablespoon fresh, chopped dill
1 tablespoon chopped fresh chives
Juice of 1/2 lemon
2 garlic cloves, minced (or 1 teaspoon garlic powder)
1 teaspoon dried Italian herbs
1/8 teaspoon salt
1 tablespoon coconut or olive oil

## Instructions:

Preheat oven to 475 degrees. Line a large rimmed baking sheet with aluminum foil, and grease with oil.

To prepare the sweet potato fries, cut the sweet potatoes into thin strips (leaving the skin on lets them get crunchy).

Mix together the salt, pepper, garlic powder, and olive oil. Toss the sweet potato strips in the spice mixture.

Spread the sweet potatoes evenly on the prepared pan. Bake for 20 minutes. Remove from the oven, turn the fries, and return to the oven to bake for an additional 10 minutes. Serve warm.

To prepare the burgers, place the meat in a bowl, and add the dill, chives, lemon juice, garlic, Italian herbs, and salt. Combine with your hands. (The mixture will be wet because of the lemon juice, but this helps the turkey or chicken stay moist during cooking.)

Heat a skillet over medium-high heat and add the oil.

Mold the meat mixture into 4 or 5 patties, and add them to the pan. Cook on one side for 5 minutes, then flip and cook on the second side for 4 to 5 minutes.

## DAY 19

### PRAYER FOR THE TABLE

*Jesus, we are here again, and we are so grateful! Thank you for bringing us back around the table to share in fellowship and nourishment. Please fill us up as we gather. So many of us are empty after the long day. Allow us to enter the night with hope and joy.*

### QUESTIONS FOR THE TABLE

1. What is one thing you love having at the table during a meal? It might be candles or flowers or cloth napkins.

2. What is one thing you can place on your table that can remind you and your family that the table is a safe and inviting place? We have a printout with a favorite quote above our table, but it can be as simple as something your family loves like seashells or a cloth-lined basket to remember communion. Get creative! It's a great visual reminder for every time you come to the table.

3. Why is it important to you to gather around the table for a meal consistently?

## RECIPE FOR THE TABLE

## STUFFED BUTTERNUT SQUASH

Serves 4.

### Ingredients:
1 butternut squash
1 tablespoon coconut oil or olive oil
1/2 red onion, chopped
1 apple, cored and chopped
1 tablespoon butter
2 garlic cloves, chopped
1 pound ground turkey (or ground chicken or ground pork)
1 teaspoon salt
1/2 teaspoon pepper
1/4 teaspoon crushed red pepper
1 teaspoon chopped fresh sage
Grated Parmesan cheese (optional)

### Instructions:
Preheat the oven to 400 degrees. Line a rimmed baking sheet or glass baking dish with aluminum foil, and grease with oil or butter.

Cut the squash in half lengthwise with a sharp knife. Place the squash, cut side down, on the prepared pan. Bake for 30 minutes. Remove from the oven, and allow to cool.

Reduce the oven temperature to 350 degrees.

Heat the oil in a skillet. Add the onion and apple. Cook, stirring, for about 3 minutes. Add the butter to give it a nice caramelization. Cook, stirring, for another 2 minutes or until the onions are translucent. Add the garlic, and cook for 1 minute. Add the ground turkey, salt, pepper, and crushed red pepper. Cook until the meat is no longer pink, about 10 minutes.

When the squash is done, remove it from the oven, and scoop out all the seeds. Remove the flesh from the squash, and place in a bowl. Leave some of the flesh on the walls of the squash to maintain its structure.

Mash the squash in the bowl with a fork, and add the fresh sage. Add this mixture to the ground turkey in the skillet. Stir until combined. Taste and add more salt or pepper if needed.

Scoop the turkey mixture into the hollow butternut squash halves. Top with the Parmesan cheese, if using. Place the filled squash halves in a baking dish, and return to the oven for 10 minutes. Cut the squash in half crosswise to make 4 servings.

## DAY 20

### PRAYER FOR THE TABLE

*Jesus, thank you for creating community and for allowing us to walk through this life with others. Thank you that we can bear one another's burdens, rejoice with one another, and hold hope for others. Impress on us how you lived your life on this earth as we gather together and break bread.*

## QUESTIONS FOR THE TABLE

1. Is it easy for you or more difficult for you to be at the table with lots of people? There is not a wrong or bad answer to this question; we are all made differently. It is good to know how you and your family operate when it comes to bringing others to the table.

2. Is there a neighbor you haven't yet invited to your table? How can your family reach out to him or her?

3. What is one way you hope to demonstrate Jesus' love to newcomers in your home?

## RECIPE FOR THE TABLE

## CHICKEN "NOODLE" SOUP

Serves 5 to 6.

### Ingredients:
1 tablespoon coconut oil or olive oil
3 carrots, chopped
3 ribs celery, chopped
1 small onion, chopped
2 garlic cloves, chopped
2 to 3 cups shredded, cooked chicken
1 teaspoon dried oregano
2 teaspoons salt
1/2 teaspoon pepper
6 cups chicken broth or stock
3 sprigs fresh thyme
1 bay leaf
2 zucchini

## Instructions:

Place the coconut oil in a soup pot, and heat over medium-high heat. Add the carrots, celery, onion, and garlic, and cook, stirring, for 5 minutes or until the onions start to become translucent but not browned.

Add the chicken, oregano, salt, and pepper, and stir to coat the chicken and veggies with the seasonings. Add the chicken broth, and top with the sprigs of thyme and bay leaf.

Bring to a boil, reduce the heat to medium-low, and simmer for 15 minutes.

While this is simmering prepare your "noodles." You can make them with your spiral vegetable slicer or with a julienne peeler. To create with a julienne peeler, take one zucchini and cut off the ends. Set the zucchini on the counter lengthwise, and drag the peeler across the zucchini, applying moderate pressure. Noodles before your eyes!

Add the zucchini to the soup, and simmer for another 10 minutes. Taste and add more salt or pepper if needed (this all depends on if your chicken broth was salted or not). Remove the thyme sprigs and bay leaf before serving.

NOTE: We have this soup as leftovers the next day. I was curious about the zucchini noodles being soggy or mushy, but they weren't! Still delicious.

## DAY 21

### PRAYER FOR THE TABLE

*Jesus, we believe you can use us right where you have us. We believe that we are exactly where you need us for just a time as this. May we lean into you as we long to be good stewards of this life you have graciously given us. Holy Spirit, grant us an overflow of grace and persistence as we keep showing up. May we trust in the power of what you can do at our very own dining room tables.*

## QUESTIONS FOR THE TABLE

1. What has been the most rewarding experience for you and your family after walking through this 21-Day Adventure at the Table?
2. What made this experience difficult or stressful? What are some practical ways you can overcome this in the future?
3. What are some aspects of this adventure you want to continue? (It might be continuing to schedule consistent time at the table, or asking questions, or inviting at least one couple or family a week to your table.)

## RECIPE FOR THE TABLE

## CREAMY CHICKEN PICCATA

Serves 4 to 5.

### Ingredients:

1 tablespoon coconut oil or olive oil
1/2 tablespoon butter
2 (8-ounce) boneless, skinless chicken breasts, cut in half horizontally
1 teaspoon salt
1/4 teaspoon pepper
2 garlic cloves, minced
1 1/4 cups chicken broth or stock
1/2 cup heavy whipping cream or half-and-half
1/3 cup finely grated Parmesan cheese

2 tablespoons capers, drained
Juice of 1 lemon
Cooked noodles or steamed vegetables

## Instructions:

Place a large skillet over medium-high heat, and add the oil and butter. Allow butter to melt and bubble.

Season chicken with salt and pepper.

Place the chicken in the pan, and cook until golden on each side and cooked through, 5 to 6 minutes on each side depending on the thickness of your chicken. (The chicken is fully cooked when it registers 165 degrees on a meat thermometer. To check the temperature, insert the needle of the thermometer into the thickest part of the chicken.) When the chicken is done, remove it to a plate, and tent with foil.

Add the garlic to the pan, and cook, stirring occasionally, until fragrant, about 1 minute.

Reduce the heat to medium, and add the broth and cream. Bring the sauce to a boil. Season with a dash of salt and pepper, add the Parmesan cheese and capers, and allow the sauce to simmer until it thickens, about 2 minutes.

Pour in the lemon juice. (If your family does not like lemon, use only half the juice and taste from there.) Allow to simmer for 1 minute. Taste and add any salt or additional lemon juice.

To serve, place chicken on top of noodles or steamed veggies and spoon the sauce on top.

# Appendix D

## HANDY SHOPPING LIST FOR THE

## 21-DAY ADVENTURE AT THE TABLE

This list includes all the main items you'll need for the recipes. Staples like salt, pepper, olive oil, and butter are not included in the list.

To download these shopping lists to your phone or other mobile device visit http://oursavorylife.com/come-eat-grocery-list/.

### Day 1: The Easiest and Tastiest Roast
1 (3-pound) chuck roast
1 (16-ounce) jar pepperoncinis
Garlic cloves

### Day 2: Cheesy Fontina Dip
Fontina cheese (1 1/2 pounds)
Garlic cloves
Fresh thyme leaves (1 tablespoon minced)
Fresh rosemary leaves (1 teaspoon minced)

Carrots, green apples, cauliflower, broccoli, or other veggies for
dipping

## Day 3: Easy, Delicious Bolognese Sauce with Sweet Potato Noodles

½ red onion

Ground beef, 80 percent lean (1 pound)

Garlic cloves

Dried oregano

Crushed red pepper, optional

Dry red wine or beef stock (1 ¼ cups)

1 (28-ounce) can crushed tomatoes

Tomato paste (2 tablespoons)

Heavy cream (¼ cup)

Parmesan cheese (½ cup finely grated)

1 sweet potato or 1 (16-ounce) package spaghetti noodles

## Day 4: Balsamic Glazed Pork

1 (2- to 3-pound) boneless pork tenderloin

Chicken or vegetable broth (1 cup)

Balsamic vinegar (½ cup)

Apple cider vinegar (2 tablespoons)

Honey (1 tablespoon)

Garlic cloves

1 yellow onion

Basmati rice (1 ½ cups)

Eggs (5 to 6)

## Day 5: Chicken Curry with Cauliflower Rice

2 medium onions

Garlic cloves

Fresh ginger (1 tablespoon peeled and finely minced)
Curry powder
Ground cumin
Cayenne pepper, optional
2 (8-ounce) boneless, skinless chicken breasts
1 (14.5-ounce) can diced tomatoes
Full-fat, canned coconut cream (3/4 cup)
1/4 pound cashews (1 cup)
1 head cauliflower or basmati rice
Chicken broth or stock (1/4 cup)
Garlic powder
Golden raisins (1 cup)

## Day 6: It's Done Already? Chicken Salsa Soup

White onion
Garlic cloves
Chicken broth or stock (6 cups)
2 limes
Rotisserie or precooked chicken (2 cups shredded)
1 (15-ounce) can white cannellini beans, optional
Frozen corn, optional (1 cup)
1 (16-ounce) jar tomatillo salsa
Toppings: hot sauce, sour cream, shredded Cheddar cheese, fresh
    cilantro, avocado, and limes

## Day 7: Cilantro Lime Fish Tacos

Garlic cloves
Cilantro leaves (1 cup)
2 limes
Ground cumin
1 pound mahi mahi

Corn tortillas

Toppings: sour cream, extra cilantro for garnish, salsa, limes, cheese, avocados

## Day 8: Thin Crust Pizza

Tapioca flour (1 cup)

Potato flour (1/4 cup)

Dried Italian herbs

Garlic powder

Parmesan cheese, optional (1/4 cup finely grated)

Powdered unflavored gelatin (1 teaspoon)

1 egg

Harissa oil or crushed red pepper, optional

Fleur de sel, optional

Toppings: pizza sauce, mozzarella cheese, pepperoni, bell peppers, red onions

## Day 9: White Chicken Chili

Coconut oil

1 onion

Cooked chicken (2 cups shredded)

Garlic powder

Chicken broth or stock (2 1/4 cups)

1 (15.5-ounce) can Great Northern beans

Frozen corn, optional (1 cup)

4 ounces fresh roasted and chopped green chiles (or one 4-ounce can chopped green chilies)

Ground cumin

Dried oregano

Cayenne pepper

Plain Greek yogurt (1 cup)

Heavy whipping cream (1/2 cup)

## Day 10: A Paleo Breakfast Recipe: Sweet Potato Hash

Bacon, optional (5 strips)
2 large sweet potatoes
Onion powder
Coconut oil
1 red or white onion
1/2 poblano pepper
Garlic cloves
Eggs (2 to 4)

## Day 11: The Best Burger Recipe

Worcestershire sauce
Garlic powder
Onion powder
2 1/2 pounds ground chuck, 80 percent lean
Toppings: Cheddar cheese, fresh tomatoes, red onion, avocados

## Day 12: Stuffed Bell Peppers

Coconut oil or olive oil
1 (8-ounce) package baby bella mushrooms, optional
1/2 medium red onion
1 small zucchini, optional
1 carrot, optional
1 pound ground beef, 80 percent lean
Garlic cloves
Marinara sauce (1 1/2 cups)
Handful spinach
Crushed red pepper, optional
4 bell peppers
Parmesan cheese, optional

## Day 13: Wedge Salad with Homemade Herb Dressing

3 green onions

Fresh basil leaves (1/2 cup chopped)

Fresh dill (1 tablespoon chopped)

Lemon

Dijon mustard

Garlic cloves

Plain Greek yogurt (1/2 cup)

Heavy whipping cream (1/2 cup)

Iceberg lettuce or salad greens

Cherry tomatoes

Bacon

Red onion

Shredded sharp Cheddar cheese

## Day 14: Honey Mustard Chicken Bake with Roasted Veggies

Honey (1/3 cup)

Dijon mustard (1/3 cup)

Apple cider vinegar

4 chicken thighs or 2 (8-ounce) chicken breasts

Garlic cloves

1 bunch broccoli

3 carrots

1 red onion

## Day 15: Butternut Squash Lasagna

1 red onion

1 pound ground beef, 80 percent lean

Garlic cloves

1 (24-ounce) jar marinara sauce

1 small butternut squash

1 pound fresh mozzarella

## Day 16: Chicken Pot Pie Soup

1/2 yellow onion

4 carrots

4 ribs celery

Cooked chicken or turkey (3 cups shredded) or 2 pounds chicken
    breasts

Arrowroot or cornstarch

Dried Italian herbs

Dried sage

Low-sodium chicken broth (2 1/2 cups)

Heavy whipping cream or half-and-half (1/4 cup)

Frozen peas, optional (1/2 cup)

## Day 17: Hearty Beef Chili

Bacon (4 to 5 strips)

1 red bell pepper

1 poblano pepper

1 red onion

Garlic cloves

1 jalapeño

1 1/2 pounds ground sirloin or ground beef, 80 percent lean

Tomato paste (2 tablespoons)

Chili powder

Ground cumin

Cayenne pepper

Red wine, beef stock, or beer (1/2 cup)

1 (28-ounce) can crushed tomatoes

1 (15-ounce) can black beans, optional

## Day 18: Turkey Burgers with Sweet Potato Fries

1 large or 2 small sweet potatoes

Garlic powder

1 pound ground chicken or ground turkey
Fresh dill (½ tablespoon chopped)
Fresh chives (1 tablespoon chopped)
Lemon
Garlic cloves or garlic powder
Dried Italian herbs
Coconut oil or olive oil

## Day 19: Stuffed Butternut Squash

1 butternut squash
Coconut oil or olive oil
½ red onion
1 apple
Garlic cloves
1 pound ground turkey
    (or ground chicken or ground pork)
Crushed red pepper
Fresh sage (1 teaspoon chopped)
Grated Parmesan cheese (optional)

## Day 20: Chicken "Noodle" Soup

Coconut oil or olive oil
3 carrots
3 ribs celery
1 small onion
Garlic clove
Cooked chicken (2 to 3 cups shredded)
Dried oregano
Chicken broth or stock (6 cups)
Fresh thyme (3 sprigs)
1 bay leaf
2 zucchini

## Day 21: Creamy Chicken Piccata

Coconut oil or olive oil

2 boneless, skinless chicken breasts (8 ounces each)

Garlic cloves

Chicken broth or stock (1 1/4 cups)

Heavy whipping cream or half-and-half (1/2 cup)

Parmesan cheese (1/3 cup finely grated)

Capers (2 tablespoons)

1 lemon

Noodles or vegetables

# ACKNOWLEDGMENTS

Thank you to so many of the broken, impoverished, hurting people who invited me into their lives through their stories, especially those mentioned in this book. Your generosity and love has revealed my own poverty and brokenness. You remind me how important the work at the table is—you help me to not forget why we are here. Please keep sharing your stories; I'll keep coming to the table.

Thank you to my husband, Jeremy. Remember when we sat on that couch in South Carolina all those years ago and you asked me, "Why don't you ever pursue writing a book?" And I blushed hard and said, "I can't." And then you helped me start a blog. You gave me room to write. You encouraged me to quit my career, and you let me find bravery and peace on a path that was beyond my dreams. You knew, didn't you? Thank you for always seeing me the way God does and for calling (and sometimes dragging) the amazing out of me.

To my mom: God knew exactly what he was doing when he made you my mom. Thank you for always having a place at the table prepared for me. Your meals permeate all of my childhood memories. Thank you for showing me the power of always having your door open and your pantry available. Thank you for loving me and always speaking over me, "My little Bri. She is a mover and a shaker. She's going to do amazing things."

To my dad, who can weave a story in a way that captivates a whole room and leaves everyone asking for more. I first learned the art of storytelling from you. I can't wait for my one-day-children to sit on the lap of their grandpa and hear his stories.

To my sister: First of all, I am 99.8 percent sure I am alive today because of all the times you had to rescue me as a child. Thank you for always cheering me on when I just wanted to hide under the covers. Thank you for being the first one to read the finalized book all the way through and for celebrating with me. Thank you to my brother who was always willing to test my on-the-fly recipes while I was in college and trying to figure out this cooking thing. I still owe you that hot sauce chicken quesadilla. ☺

To my Grandma Moore and Grandma Mullins: You two were going to the table and inviting the neighbors long before it was popular. You did the tireless work of feeding your people and gathering them around a table. You both may think it went unnoticed, but *I* noticed. God has used you to forever change my life.

To one of my favorites: Karla Nelson, I do not even want to think about what this journey of writing a book without you would look like. I actually do not think I could have done it without you. (I tell Jesus this often.) Or voxer. Voxer and Jesus—saving lives. ☺

Thank you to my agent Ruth Samsel. You picked me out of a crowd and saw something worthy in me before anyone else did. Thank you for believing in me and walking this journey with me.

Thank you to my editor Jessica Wong. You put my words through a refining fire and polished them until they shined. You always picked up the phone when I was ready to burn the whole thing down. Thank you. And to the amazing people at Thomas Nelson—I may have birthed this book but there is no way it was coming into the world without you. You are gracious and you are amazing.

Thank you to my team at Compassion, especially the people who have managed me over the years, Chris Giovagnoni, Dustin Hardage, Tom Emmons, and Shaun Groves. As a young woman entering her first career, you all noticed my writing and started calling it out. You were quick to believe in the work God can do through me and you created every opportunity for God to grow and shape me. There is no way I would be where I am today without all of you. Thank you.

Thank you to my Lord and Savior. Thank you for calling out the marginalized, the "least of these," the broken and lonely, and then sharing a meal with them. Your way has turned me inside out and I am all in. Please keep bringing your people to my table. I will keep feeding them.

# ABOUT THE AUTHOR

B ri McKoy is a writer and home cook. She currently serves as the visionary and leader for Compassion Bloggers, successor to Shaun Groves, connecting with bestselling authors and popular bloggers daily. She is the owner and writer for her blog OurSavoryLife.com, a food blog with recipes and stories from around her table.

Her recipes have been featured on Blendtec.com (known as the world's most advanced blender), CivilizedCavemanCooking.com (whose author has written two *New York Times* bestselling cookbooks), and Shape.com (the online home to *Shape* magazine, the second largest young women's magazine). Bri is a contributor to the award-winning Compassion International blog and to GraceTable.org, a community blog about food and faith.

She currently lives in Hermosa Beach, California, with her husband and dog. You can find her in the kitchen or in her neighborhood knocking on doors and inviting people to her table!

## COMPASSION INTERNATIONAL

Many of the stories about children living in poverty shared in *Come and Eat* are children Bri McKoy met while traveling with

Compassion. For more than eight years, Bri has traveled to the developing countries where Compassion works. She and her husband are so convinced in the work Compassion is doing that they are fierce advocates for this nonprofit. Being involved in the work God is doing through Compassion has given Bri and her husband a more clear and palpable vision for God's love for the marginalized. It has compelled them to be more involved in serving the poor and hurting.

Compassion International exists to release children from poverty in Jesus' name. It is a child-advocacy ministry that pairs compassionate people with those who are suffering from poverty. The ministry releases children from spiritual, economic, social, and physical poverty.

To partner with God and help release a child from poverty through Compassion, please visit compassion.com/comeandeat.

# NOTES

## Chapter 2: A Place for Us at the Table

1. The Six O'Clock "Scamble," LLC, "Take the Family Dinner Challenge," http://www.thescramble.com/family-dinner-challenge-statistics/.
2. Commentary of the *Faithlife Study Bible* under Luke 10:39.

## Chapter 4: A Vision for the Table

1. Barbara Kingsolver, *Animal, Vegetable, Miracle: One Year of Seasonal Eating* (New York: HarperCollins, 2007), 125.
2. Laurie Beth Jones, *The Path: Creating Your Mission Statement for Work and for Life* (New York: Hyperion, 1996), 3.

## Chapter 6: Hospitality at the Table

1. Anne Lamott's Facebook page, posted February 8, 2015, https://www.facebook.com/AnneLamott/posts/630100177119629.

## Chapter 7: Peace at the Table

1. E. R. Clendenen, "Peace," in C. Brand, C. Draper et al., eds., *Holman Illustrated Bible Dictionary* (Nashville, TN: Holman Bible Publishers, 2003), 1262.
2. Ibid.

## Chapter 9: Meekness at the Table

1. https://www.brainyquote.com/quotes/quotes/p/paulinephi160520.html.

2. Francis of Assisi quoted in Brennan Manning, *The Signature of Jesus* (New York: WaterBrook Multnomah, 1996), 86, emphasis mine.

## Chapter 10: Story at the Table

1. John Piper, "God Is Always Doing 10,000 Things in Your Life," Desiring God, http://www.desiringgod.org/articles/ every-moment-in-2013-god-will-be-doing-10–000-things-in-your-life.

## Chapter 11: Questions at the Table

1. Robert G. Rayburn II, "Salt," in J. D. Barry et al., eds., *The Lexham Bible Dictionary* (Bellingham, WA: Lexham Press, 2014), http:// www.academia.edu/10955672/_Salt_.

2. Ralph Ellis et al., "Orlando Shooting: 49 Killed, Shooter Pledged ISIS Allegiance," CNN, June 13, 2016, http://www.cnn. com/2016/06/12/us/orlando-nightclub-shooting/.

3. Hemant Mehta, "Christian Pastor Celebrates Nightclub Massacre: 'There's 50 Less Pedophiles in This World,'" *Friendly Atheist* (blog), June 12, 2016, http://www.patheos.com/blogs/ friendlyatheist/2016/06/12/christian-pastor-celebrates-nightclub-massacre-theres-50-less-pedophiles-in-this-world/.

## Chapter 12: Revolution at the Table

1. Simon Carey Holt, *Eating Heaven: Spirituality at the Table* (Moreland, Australia: Acorn Press, 2013), 150.

2. Michael Frost, *Surprise the World: The Five Habits of Highly Missional People* (Colorado Springs, CO: Navpress, 2015), 9.

3. Ibid.

4. Ibid.